BOOST

Your
Nursing
Leadership
Career

BOOST

Your
Nursing
Leadership
Career

50
Lessons
That Drive
Success

Kenneth R. White
Dorrie K. Fontaine

ACHE Management Series

Your board, staff, or clients may also benefit from this book's insight. For more information on quantity discounts, contact the Health Administration Press Marketing Manager at (312) 424-9450.

This publication is intended to provide accurate and authoritative information in regard to the subject matter covered. It is sold, or otherwise provided, with the understanding that the publisher is not engaged in rendering professional services. If professional advice or other expert assistance is required, the services of a competent professional should be sought.

The statements and opinions contained in this book are strictly those of the author(s) and do not represent the official positions of the American College of Healthcare Executives or the Foundation of the American College of Healthcare Executives.

21   20   19   18   17   5   4   3   2   1

Library of Congress Cataloging-in-Publication Data
Names: White, Kenneth R. (Kenneth Ray), 1956– author. | Fontaine, Dorrie K.,
    author.
Title: Boost your nursing leadership career : 50 lessons that drive success /
    Kenneth R. White and Dorrie K. Fontaine.
Description: Chicago, IL : HAP, [2017] | Series: ACHE management series
Identifiers: LCCN 2016058473 (print) | LCCN 2017002381 (ebook) | ISBN
    9781567938869 (alk. paper) | ISBN 9781567938890 (xml) | ISBN 9781567938906
    (epub) | ISBN 9781567938913 (mobi)
Subjects: LCSH: Nursing services—Administration. | Leadership.
Classification: LCC RT89 .W48 2017 (print) | LCC RT89 (ebook) | DDC
    362.17/3068—dc23
LC record available at https://lccn.loc.gov/2016058473

The paper used in this publication meets the minimum requirements of American National Standard for Information Sciences—Permanence of Paper for Printed Library Materials, ANSI Z39.48-1984. ∞ ™

Acquisitions editor: Janet Davis; Project editor: Andrew Baumann; Cover designer: Brad Norr; Layout: PerfecType

Found an error or a typo? We want to know! Please e-mail it to hapbooks@ache.org, mentioning the book's title and putting "Book Error" in the subject line.

For photocopying and copyright information, please contact Copyright Clearance Center at www.copyright.com or at (978) 750-8400.

Health Administration Press
A division of the Foundation of the American
    College of Healthcare Executives
One North Franklin Street, Suite 1700
Chicago, IL 60606–3529
(312) 424–2800

To our teachers, students, and colleagues—past, present, and future—and all the lessons you've taught us. To the joy of being nurses and contributing to a profession that provides endless opportunities for leadership and improvement of patient care.

Contents

Acknowledgments

THIS BOOK IS a vision that grew out of another book that Ken wrote with Steve Lindsey—*Take Charge of Your Healthcare Management Career: 50 Lessons That Drive Success*—which aimed to help newer generations of healthcare executives succeed. We are indebted to Steve Lindsey for his early vision of such a book and are grateful to him for his perennial passion to improve patient care.

Each of the 50 lessons in this book starts with a quote from a successful nurse leader whom we believe to be an expert on the subject of the lesson. We owe a debt of gratitude to the nurses who gave of their time and expertise to review the lessons and provide quotes. Many improvements resulted from their input.

We are grateful to Janet Davis, our acquisitions editor at Health Administration Press. She believed in us, encouraged us to stretch, and supported us every step of the way in developing a book for nurse leaders at all stages of their career—from charge nurse to chief executive officer or academic dean and university president. We are also grateful to Andrew Baumann, editorial production manager at Health Administration Press, for his keen eye for detail and to all of the other Health Administration Press team members who contributed to producing and promoting this new book.

I (Ken) would like to thank two early role models and a career mentor. I started my nursing career in 1973 as an orderly at Okmulgee Memorial Hospital in Oklahoma, where my first supervisor and role model was Carol Rogers. My second job, which put me through college, was at Saint Francis Hospital in Tulsa, Oklahoma, where I was an orthopedic technician; my nurse manager there, Dorothy

Doll, was not only a role model but also a coach and champion of my career. The career mentor who helped me realize my goals and who encouraged me to pursue nursing as a nontraditional student was Dr. Jim Begun. Jim was my doctoral dissertation director as well as a friend and colleague. He not only encouraged me to pursue a nursing education but also was a mentor for my scholarly work, which has focused on the future of the nursing profession. Without Jim as my champion, I daresay I would have had a far more difficult time pursuing my passion. I also thank my husband, Dr. Carl Outen, for his support, encouragement, and patience while I was writing the book. I am grateful to my coauthor, Dorrie Fontaine, dean of the School of Nursing at the University of Virginia, who has been a loyal supporter, colleague, and friend and under whose vision and leadership I have been allowed to grow professionally; Dorrie has always encouraged me to "be the best Ken I can be." Sister Julie Hyer, OP, has been a steadfast friend and mentor since 1980; she has provided counsel and ideas and has served as a sounding board. Finally, for more than 20 years, Dr. Norma Geddes has inspired me "to follow my bliss."

I (Dorrie) thank my role models throughout four decades of critical care and academic nursing. They have been clinical nurse specialists, nurse managers, chief nursing officers, and academic faculty and deans. Many of these treasured colleagues provided lead quotes for our lessons here. The best leadership experience I acquired was through working with the American Association of Critical-Care Nurses and with Dean Emerita Kathy Dracup at the University of California, San Francisco. The day I met Ken White (when he was a nurse practitioner student at the University of Virginia) was one of the happiest days in my career, because he later agreed to join the School of Nursing as an associate dean. He has been instrumental in creating joy in the workplace for me and for others every day. Finally, I thank my husband, Barry Fontaine, who celebrates nursing every day by providing a home where all of our nursing friends, faculty, staff, and students are welcomed, as well as our son, Sumner, now an attorney, who has always been a leader in so many memorable ways. I will always be grateful for their support.

Introduction

It goes without saying that no perfect job exists. No organization, group of people, or position on earth comes without some measure of challenges, problems, and messiness. But there are ways to deal with the world's near-constant imperfections, particularly in the workplace, and certain universal truths make it possible to find best practices and answers. So with those observations in mind, and with more than eight decades of professional experience between us, we have compiled 50 lessons to steer you thoughtfully, carefully, and with poise and grace toward, onto, and along your chosen career path as a nurse leader.

This book takes a three-pronged approach to introducing nurses to what it takes to be leaders and how to go about developing one's career. The organization of the book into a trio of themes—Manage Yourself, Manage Your Job, and Boost Your Career—is based on the refrains we have heard from nurses at all stages of their careers who have wondered what skills they need to be a successful nurse leader. Most of us can benefit from recalibrations such as returning to basic self-awareness; fervently desiring to make things better; learning to pay attention to what matters most; and matching our gifts, talents, and experience with the right organization and role.

Life, work, and everything in between should be informed by these ideas. Those who dismiss them likely will not perform well or contribute to their organization's mission, vision, and values. They may be overlooked for promotions and find it difficult to move elsewhere, even laterally. They may be outsourced, outmoded, and outmaneuvered by others.

Success isn't something you're born with; it is carefully cultivated, mastered, and honed. The most successful nurse leaders have learned that authenticity and truthfulness are the best path, and they have learned to *really* pay attention, to *truly* be consummate professionals, and to *wholly* be the very best version of themselves that they can be. The traits, lessons, and skills outlined in this book must be mastered for maximum personal and career success.

We all have dream jobs—those positions that lie at the intersection of our gifts, our passions, and the needs of society. When it works well, a job can fit like a glove and be satisfying to your very core. We hope that this book and its lessons will help you find the kind of professional joy you're seeking.

We wish you the best.

Ken White and Dorrie Fontaine
Charlottesville, Virginia

SECTION I

Manage Yourself

WHY START A book on careers with a section on how to manage yourself? It's always best, as Glinda the Good Witch says in *The Wizard of Oz*, to start at the beginning. If you can't manage yourself, you can't tackle all the things that come next: people and budgets, the complaint of a patient's family, or your own business. If you don't have a realistic picture of your strengths, gifts, and talents or don't know what you need to learn and how to present yourself as a professional, you can't make your very best leap out of the starting gate.

Of course, plenty of people don't follow the lessons that are detailed in this section. They're the colleagues who have never cultivated an interest in others and remain self-focused; the managers who are so risk averse that they're ineffective; the individuals who overly rely on technology for their presentations, then hit snags and become utterly derailed; the people who misuse social media to their detriment or who cast blame rather than own their mistakes; and those whose speech, writing, and presentation skills lull audiences into a stupor.

Those who aren't familiar with lessons 1–18 sometimes commit gaffes that are almost too bad to be true—for example, the graduate student who sent her job application in a mailing tube with her resume on pink scented paper, a glamour shot picture, and a return e-mail address that contained the word *diva*; the former colleague who, although smart and well educated, talked too familiarly and revealed too much; the peer who whined, complained, and always lamented why something *couldn't* be done and who wondered why people avoided her; or the practitioner who was so burned out that he brought others—including his patients—down with him.

These individuals never bothered to look at themselves to figure out why others reacted to them so strongly, why they remained ineffective in their jobs, why colleagues avoided them, and why, ultimately, their positions were eliminated or they were fired. They didn't take the time to manage *themselves* first.

When you manage *yourself* and cultivate the best *you* there is, good things happen. You become like the hospital CEO who visited us in a hospital other than his own when we were ill; like the colleagues who jotted notes of thanks to us for small things, tucking them in our mailboxes or under our doors; like the coworkers who sent food, flowers, or cards when a relative died; and like those who listened intently, compassionately, and with the kind of interest that today is all too rare.

So much of who we are at a job begins with who and how we are as humans. It's important to know what to do and what not to do—and although some lessons in this section may seem obvious, they're important enough to spell out explicitly. The lessons for success in this section will get you off to a good start in boosting your career.

Establish a Life Vision

*Your vision for your career should reflect a deep understanding
that you exist in an imperfect world of struggles and possibilities.
Hopefully, your vision will be framed by your passion for turning
those possibilities into realities.*

—Diana Mason, PhD, RN, FAAN, professor emerita,
Hunter College School of Nursing, New York City,
and past president (2013–2015), American Academy of Nursing

So you've got the academic training, your degree(s), a license,
and perhaps a residency or certification behind you—and you have
the hunger for a life-changing career in nursing. Now's the perfect
time to establish a personal vision statement for your career—just
as though you were developing a campaign or slogan to market a
company's assets, except that it's all about *you*.

It's crucial to begin your professional nursing journey by taking
an honest look at yourself—what you like, what your strengths are,
what others say about you—and then mapping out a series of goals
to declare a vision for your professional life. Jotting down notes is a
good way to begin. These notes don't have to be formal or intensive,
but spend some time and thought on them. Following are a few
questions to consider to get you started:

- What do I value most?
- How do I like to spend my day?
- What have others told me I'm good at? What do *I* consider my strengths to be?
- How do I want to make a difference in the world?
- Where do I want to be in 5, 10, or 20 years?
- What's my ideal job, and where is it located?
- What sort of leader do I want to be?
- How do I want to be remembered?

Don't rely exclusively on outside sources for advice that will determine your future—look inside yourself. Ask yourself what makes you happy. Record your thoughts over time, and you may find a path for your career. *You* may have the best career advice in your soul.

Bear in mind that your personal vision statement is a fluid document. You're not bound to it; you can change it as you see fit. As you progress in your career, different ideas will occur to you—new or additional educational goals, hopes for geographic change, decisions to broaden your experience in one direction versus another—so it's wise to keep your personal vision statement up to date as your thoughts about your trajectory shift.

Like a physical exam or dental checkup, schedule regular meetings with yourself to consider (or reconsider) your vision statement. From time to time, make sure it still works for you.

EXERCISE 1

Think of some defining moments in your life—times, choices, or situations that have defined who you are today. For each defining moment, articulate how it shaped your values. How do these instances inform your life vision? What will you be doing, and what impact do you want to make on the world in, say, 20 years?

EXERCISE 2

It's the day of your funeral. Three people will each deliver a short eulogy on your life and the impact you made. One will offer thoughts on your work life, one will share memories of your family and friends, and one will speak about your contribution to the world. What do you hope they will say?

RESOURCES

Palmer, P. J. 2009. *A Hidden Wholeness: The Journey Toward an Undivided Life.* San Francisco: Jossey-Bass.

———. 2000. *Let Your Life Speak: Listening for the Voice of Vocation.* San Francisco: Jossey-Bass.

Get Comfortable with Risk

Even confident people have doubts when encountering new opportunities. You may think, "I haven't done this before—can I succeed?" Take stock of your strengths, and if they fit the critical needs of the situation, forge ahead. Focus on what you do know and cover your weaknesses by soliciting advice from others who have experience in areas where you don't.

—Teresa DiMarco, BSN, MBA, managing director and cofounder, River Crossing Advisors, Richmond, Virginia, and former CEO of several technology-enabled healthcare services companies

DURING MILITARY TRAINING, a sergeant will scream, "Make a decision, lieutenant!" What the sergeant means is: Gather as many facts as possible in the time you have and then give it your best shot—because lives may be at stake. This is a call to action.

The call translates to civilian life, too. Be prepared to take a few big risks in your career, particularly early on. Think about moving into a nontraditional leadership position or starting a company as a nurse entrepreneur. Many successful nurse leaders began their professional lives by taking a job that stretched their capabilities and found that the process ultimately advanced their careers.

Note that, in this fast-paced world, doing nothing is inherently risky. We often consider the risks and consequences of our actions, but we should also remember that the status quo and inaction also carry huge risks.

Uncertainties are a necessary part of any job—and to be a successful nurse leader, you will need to be comfortable with taking risks. It's simply a fact that those who learn to take calculated risks that align with their organization's goals and vision will achieve better results throughout their career. The safe road may feel more comfortable, but change is the only constant in healthcare organizations—and all healthcare organizations are looking for leaders who can get results. That means mastering the route to change.

Taking risks, however, does not mean acting recklessly. Think about what will happen *after* you take the leap, whatever it might be. Talk to people you trust, and get their take. Make sure you have both capital and time enough to pivot onto the next project, should things go awry. Weigh the chances of success and make sure you have what you need to make your leap a success. With all that in place, you are ready to take a risk.

Successful entrepreneurs sometimes advise, "Fail small and fail fast." When you first observe a problem, think of it as an opportunity. Ask yourself how you can solve it and what product or procedure might be part of the solution.

Also remember the value in speaking up. When your team is struggling with a problem, do you offer the solution that you have been considering? Or do you hold back and wait for someone else to suggest it? Many former executives say that their only regrets center around not being more forceful and vocal in offering their opinions and ideas when faced with seemingly insurmountable problems. Speaking up is essential, even if your idea doesn't seem fully conceived.

Note that many executives tend to overestimate risk when they maneuver into new or unknown areas. Fear of failure and fear of the unknown can lead to inaction precisely when action is what's required.

As you weigh your options, remember: No decision has a 100 percent guaranteed chance of success, but standing still in healthcare is never an option, either.

Here are steps to follow when taking risks:

1. **Understand exactly what problem you're trying to solve.** Spend time defining the central problem or issue.
2. **Gather information and facts about the problem.** Once the problem has been determined, gather information. Talk to people about the problem, and listen carefully. Discuss and analyze potential solutions in a thoughtful, organized way.
3. **Identify the best course of action.** Once potential solutions have been considered, decide who should have a hand in solving it. What do they see as the best possible solution? Listen carefully and thoughtfully, and be amenable to tweaking the solution based on what others advise.
4. **Consider the possible outcomes or consequences of your risk.** What's the best result your decision might bring? What's the worst? Learn to project scenarios that may unfold from your decision, and consider legal, budgetary, and regulatory issues.
5. **Go for it.** When you have about 80 percent of your questions answered, take the risk. In the risk's early days, take time to analyze the results.
6. **Encourage others on your staff to take risks, too.** Doing so will instill a level of strategic thinking in your organization's culture.

Those who offer solutions and are not afraid to do so develop a reputation as problem solvers—the kind of people whom health-care organizations value highly. Although you will make mistakes, you can learn from them to improve your rate of success. Remind yourself that you are in the healthcare field to make a difference, solve problems, and improve things. Be that leader who gets things done—not the one who gets outmoded because you kept silent at a critical juncture.

EXERCISE 1

Whether it's a household, personal, or work problem, set a goal to understand and devise a solution to an issue that you currently face within the next 30 days.

EXERCISE 2

Keep a personal journal of your decisions. Assign a risk to each decision you make. Later, go back and evaluate your decisions. What could you have done to improve your chances for success? Periodically review your journal. Are you improving in your ability to assess problems and take risks?

RESOURCE

Clark, B., and S. Lindsey. 2013. "Success Requires Risk: 5 Ways Health System Leaders Should Undertake Risk and Uncertainty to Succeed." *Becker's Hospital Review*. Published November 25. www.beckershospitalreview.com/hospital-management -administration/success-requires-risk-5-ways-health-system -leaders-should-undertake-risk-and-uncertainty-to-succeed.html.

Focus Your Time

Given the complexity of the current healthcare landscape, a leader with a large span of control can easily be responsible for overseeing dozens of projects that are all "important." As a leader, you must manage your energy because time is a finite resource. I often evaluate and prioritize initiatives in the context of the Institute for Healthcare Improvement's Triple Aim. I ask myself, "Is this an initiative that will improve quality and satisfaction, improve the health of our patient population, and reduce costs?" Choosing the right work to invest your energy in is critical for the effective management of time.

—Stephan Davis, DNP, MHSA, RN, CPHQ, NEA-BC, FACHE, director of academic partnerships, WellStar Health System, Marietta, Georgia

A MAJOR THIEF of your success is inappropriate management of your time. What does wasted time look like? Like a lot of things you see every day in offices across America: Pointless hallway conversations. Aimless Internet surfing. Procrastination. Texting with friends and family. Failing to manage your electronic files and having a disorganized, jumbled computer desktop. Long lunches without a work focus.

You can lose time in other, not so obvious ways. Time can be wasted by taking on too much or by planning unrealistic project deadlines. Because time is money, as they say, and something you need to build your career, perhaps the most subtle time waster is working on things that will not give you the best return.

Daniel Goleman, author of *Focus: The Hidden Driver of Excellence*, asserts that our digital era has caused us to be more engaged with machines than with the people around us—a circumstance that has also blunted our ability to pay attention and maintain focus. Attention is a critical ingredient in managing your time; you need it to prioritize your projects, to zero in on the tasks in front of you, and to fully deliver on your promises and expectations. Without it, you're just another time waster, and the world is rife with those.

So what can you do to best manage your time?

- **Practice being focused and attentive.** Tackling a task that requires lengthy, sustained attention—or listening thoughtfully to a colleague or your spouse—is a great way to sharpen this skill, which is a critical first step to fighting off time wasters.
- **Limit your goals.** Focus your (and your team's) energy on a few important projects and goals that you can execute well. Don't volunteer to take on new projects or goals that are so many or so diverse that you can't do any of them well. Choose a few, if you're able, and dig in so that you can knock them out of the park.
- **Be organized from the get-go.** Although metal filing cabinets have today been replaced by computers, many people's electronic files are as messy, poorly organized, and difficult to navigate as those hulking rows of steel. Is your desktop littered with old, useless photos and files that need to be trashed? Do you have hundreds of thousands of old e-mails from years back? Take the time to clean up. Develop a system to file, back up, and share information. Nothing is more maddening—or a bigger waste of your time—than not being able to locate what you need when you need it. Develop a system to organize yourself at the project's start.

- **Teach, empower, and delegate.** The old adage "If you want something done right, do it yourself" is a time waster. Teaching others how to handle a task may require more time up front, but empowering them by delegating is key to effective time management. Showing confidence in others by delegating important projects to them is also a natural means of cultivating loyalty and trust among your colleagues and employees. If you're surrounded by capable people, they'll be glad for your vote of confidence and will likely be eager to please you.
- **Group similar activities together during your day, and set a limited amount of time to work on them.** Schedule regular slots of time to check e-mail, return phone calls, work on particular projects, and make rounds. Always carry a notepad or electronic device when away from your desk so that you can jot down notes and reminders to yourself. However, don't become a slave to your device in the name of being organized. Know when to put it down so that you can, as a nurse leader, be attuned and attentive to your many stakeholders.
- **Understand that complications and disruptions happen.** In healthcare, no day goes exactly according to plan. However, you can accommodate the inevitable ups and downs by planning in advance. Assign yourself "soft" deadlines. If a report is due on May 15, aim to finish it by May 1. That will give you adequate time to deal with any disruptions that may crop up.
- **Focus on activities that add value to your organization's mission.** Generally, for healthcare organizations, value is related to improving patients' health and sustaining the health of caregivers. As you lead meetings, read e-mails, and write reports, ask yourself how these activities contribute—in ways big and small, direct and indirect—to the overall mission of your organization. That alone will give you a sense of what is

truly important in your work and what deserves most of your attention.

EXERCISE 1

Divide your tasks into a half dozen or so subject areas, with general descriptions that reflect your role and responsibilities in your organization (e.g., meetings, correspondence, finances, special projects, human resources), then keep track of how you spend your day in each area. As you log your day, acknowledge what might be improved by identifying the thieves of your time. At the end of the day, how can you be a better steward of your time—and thus of your career?

EXERCISE 2

Using Stephen Covey's book *The 7 Habits of Highly Effective People*, identify what is urgent or important, and reprioritize your daily activities.

RESOURCES

Birkinshaw, J., and J. Cohen. 2013. "Make Time for the Work That Matters." *Harvard Business Review* 91 (9): 115–18.

Covey, S. R. 2013. *The 7 Habits of Highly Effective People: Powerful Lessons in Personal Change,* anniversary edition. New York: Simon & Schuster.

Duhigg, C. 2012. *The Power of Habit: Why We Do What We Do in Life and Business.* New York: Random House.

Goleman, D. 2013. *Focus: The Hidden Driver of Excellence.* New York: HarperCollins.

Adopt Appreciative Practice

Learning to be a leader is a lifelong journey that requires embracing and embodying appreciative practice. Appreciative practice is focusing on the positive to bring out the best in ourselves, those we lead, and everyone around us. It allows us to form a collective dream and to bring that dream into reality by honoring all the good things and strengths that we as a team want to bring with us into the future. As leaders and as human beings, it is our ethical responsibility to bring out the best in others, leverage their strengths to propel innovation, and think beyond the possible by engaging in positive dialogue to inspire collective action for a better world.

—Joan M. Vitello-Cicciu, PhD, RN, NEA-BC, FAHA, FAAN, dean, Graduate School of Nursing, University of Massachusetts Medical School, Worcester

ALL TOO OFTEN, we come home at the end of a long and stressful day, and the evening's dinner conversation focuses on all the things that went wrong. We hone in on the negative without considering all the positive things that happened—the day's bright spots, the meetings that went well, the people who brought us happiness. Taking a step back to understand the concept of *mindfulness*—a catchall term that basically means focusing on what really matters—encourages an inward approach as we make sense of the world around us. Adopting appreciative practice is a route to mindfulness—and a real pathway to positivity.

Some nurse leaders begin their one-on-one and group meetings with a question: "Can you think of something that has happened since our last meeting that makes you proud?" This is called an *appreciative check-in*. Early on, the exercise might feel awkward because staff may not be accustomed to this celebratory opener. Some people might not want to self-identify points of pride because it seems like bragging. Others might simply be embarrassed to be put on the spot. But when colleagues are given the opportunity to share what has made them proud, even if some opt to remain silent, the tradition often becomes everyone's favorite part of the meeting. Appreciative practice may be an individual choice—a tactic you can use at the meetings you run—or it may be an integral part of an organization's culture.

Research has repeatedly established a link between healthcare workers' mindful practices and their ability to provide competent, compassionate patient care. Tend the caregiver, it is said, and you ultimately tend the patient, too. Appreciative practice works in much the same way. If you practice positivity, you grease your cognitive circuitry in that area, making it an easier, more familiar technique to which you'll return. However brief those shared moments of pride are in the overall context of your two-hour-long meeting, appreciative practice helps you to begin on an up beat, to be present and attentive, and to connect with others in addition to strengthening those positive neurological circuits in your brain.

Appreciative practice begins by asking those present, "What is going well? For what or whom are you grateful?" At times, allowing moments of silence between each staffer's reflection is useful because it magnifies the positive and enables you and your team to adopt a more mindful approach. Permit time for everyone to speak if they'd like, and respectfully support those who wish to pass. As silly as it might feel initially, appreciative practice is a great way to start meetings. Even the hardest-hearted naysayer will be a believer before long.

Appreciative practice works by yourself, too. Asking yourself the following questions is a good way to begin your own personal appreciative practice:

- Whom do I appreciate today?
- For whom am I grateful, and why?
- Who are the organization's unsung heroes, the inconspicuous ones who work competently and diligently behind the scenes?
- How can I be wholly present, fully devoting my attention to the person in front of me? How can I connect with the person and not just the person's role in the organization?

Your own appreciative practice might also cultivate habits such as the following:

- **Sending personal notes or verbally expressing appreciation to people.** An expression of thanks might take the form of a brief e-mail, a handwritten note left on a desk, or a face-to-face comment. The important thing is to do it and to make such recognitions a habit.
- **Keeping a gratitude journal.** Jot down thoughts about the people and things you're grateful for and why. Or, simply list what rises to the top each day.
- **Scheduling regular alone time for yourself to reflect on what you are grateful for.** Whether you set aside 15 to 30 minutes in the morning to watch the sun rise while sipping your coffee or you turn off the radio on the way to work, make it a priority to channel your thoughts toward gratitude.
- **Improving your listening skills.** Good leaders listen first. Be present, and offer your full, unfettered attention to the individuals who are speaking. When they have finished speaking, repeat what they said back to them and then thoughtfully reply.

EXERCISE 1

Identify three or four of the most important "turning points" that have led you to where you are now—serendipitous moments or opportunities that turned your career in a different direction. Reflect on these turning points and write about them in your journal.

EXERCISE 2

Make it a habit to start each meeting with an appreciative check-in. Ask, "What made you proud since we last met? What is going well? Whom or what do you appreciate?"

RESOURCES

Harmon, R. B., D. K. Fontaine, M. Plews-Ogan, and A. Williams. 2012. "Achieving Transformational Change: Using Appreciative Inquiry for Strategic Planning in a School of Nursing." *Journal of Professional Nursing* 28 (2): 119–24.

May, N., D. Becker, R. Frankel, J. Haizlip, R. Harmon, M. Plews-Ogan, J. Schorling, A. Williams, and D. Whitney. 2012. *Appreciative Inquiry in Healthcare*. Brunswick, OH: Crown Custom Publishing.

University of Virginia School of Medicine Center for Appreciative Practice. 2016. "Changing the Conversation in Healthcare." Accessed October 17. https://med.virginia.edu /appreciative-practice/.

Define and Recalibrate Expectations

Believe in what you expect of others, stay the course, and model the behaviors you anticipate. With these ingredients, your expectations will be realized.

—Joan Shinkus Clark, DNP, RN, CENP, NEA-BC, FACHE, FAAN, senior vice president and chief nurse executive, Texas Health Resources, Arlington, Texas, and president (2016–2017), American Organization of Nurse Executives

AN *EXPECTATION* IS commonly defined as a belief that something will happen. You expect the sun to rise. You expect children to grow. You expect your paycheck to arrive.

But in business, including healthcare, expectations are much more than passive observations about the world or events that simply happen with the passage of time. And being passive about your own expectations—thinking "Whatever will be, will be," for example—is a sure route to lukewarm leadership and tepid success.

Having expectations—and developing, refining, and recalibrating them—is an active, engaged process. All healthcare leaders should set expectations for themselves and then actually believe they will happen. If you believe something will happen, you take positive steps in that direction. The most successful leaders know and understand the power of positive thinking.

Have you ever found yourself accommodating a drop in your own personal standards in the name of getting things done? Perhaps you were part of a work group that had poor leadership or were a member of a losing team. As the group's expectations weaken, individual members naturally experience a similar drop in their standards.

Here is where true leaders can set themselves apart. If you observe or feel an expectation slipping, you must stop the slide. Reestablish what your goals and standards are and where you're headed. You may even need to separate yourself from others who exert a negative influence on you. If possible, ally yourself with teammates and mentors who have a positive outlook and similarly high expectations. That way, you'll know you're in sync.

A good way to hone your expectations is to ask yourself a few questions:

- What would I like to see happen?
- How can I positively affect outcomes?
- Who are my best allies?
- When should work begin?
- What are the first steps I need to take to ensure a good result?

It goes without saying that to achieve your expectations, you should always offer your very best work. But how, exactly, do you do your best? One way is to seek out good mentors and model your behavior and strategies on theirs. Another is to study successful people: Find out who has achieved success in your industry and examine the way they've approached problems, large or small. See if you can figure out the ingredients to their success.

As a leader, you will discover that not everyone will agree with your approach or share your motivation and savvy. Many brilliant, motivated people fail miserably as leaders because they lack the ability to motivate others. Great leaders understand that different people have different gifts, and they manage to assemble teams that maximize each member's strengths to contribute most effectively. Great leaders meet people, accept who they are, and draw out the best in each one.

Constantly set "stretch" goals: Challenge yourself to do and be better. Above all, hone in on goals that are aligned with those of your organization, and maintain high expectations while tackling them. People like to be part of an organization that is visionary and thinks beyond the ordinary. So have those lofty personal expectations, and share your views about why and how great things can—and will—happen as you work with your colleagues.

Big, meaty efforts take time and energy, of course. They require attention, too. Be practical enough to complete the work that is important each day. Your work shouldn't consist only of easy tasks or projects born of half-conceived ideas, of course, but focusing your efforts on what *can* be done today will yield dividends tomorrow and in the weeks and years to come. Accomplishments have a way of naturally multiplying, especially under the pleasing glow of success.

EXERCISE 1

List five factors critical to your organization's success, and then write down how those issues will look ten years down the road. Ask yourself the following questions:

- What would I like to see happen?
- How can I positively affect outcomes?
- What are the first steps I should take to ensure a positive outcome?
- Who are the best people to help me achieve this outcome?
- When should work begin?

EXERCISE 2

Pick a goal—personal or professional—that you have dreamed about but never tried to accomplish. Write it down. Define the goal and begin taking steps to accomplish it. Break it down into weekly action points, and check your progress each week.

RESOURCE

Manzoni, J.-F., and J.-L. Barsoux. 1998. "The Set-Up-to-Fail Syndrome." *Harvard Business Review* 76 (2): 101–13.

Be Interested in Others

Throughout your career as a nurse leader, you will realize just how little you can accomplish alone. The sooner you learn this humbling lesson, the better. Creating meaningful relationships in your organization should be a top priority. These relationships will be key to organizing and motivating your team to accomplish your organization's goals.

—Zach McCluskey, MHA, RN, FACHE, chief executive officer, HCA Johnston-Willis Hospital, Richmond, Virginia

NURSING LEADERSHIP IS more than a job; it's a true calling. Few other vocations exist that so directly affect communities and people. And because nursing is a highly regarded, noble field, nurse executives occupy a privileged position at the helm. The best nurse executives feel an intense responsibility to learn about their community's needs and then guide their organization to respond to those needs. But this is a tall order, and only the very best succeed.

With the introduction of endless sorts of technological devices, however—not to mention our modern predilection to share overly intimate details on the Internet and to spend every otherwise unoccupied moment fiddling with electronic devices—a new, unhealthy era of intense self-focus has arisen. Our collective attention span has atrophied. Coupled with the nation's growing self-absorption, the notions that "everyone deserves a prize" and "no one should be singled out for special treatment" have yielded a common and sometimes overwhelming sense of entitlement. "You can do or be anything you want" and "The sky's the limit" are frequent words of encouragement. Although these sentiments may have some validity, no one who is truly successful got anywhere without a lot of hard work, determination, and the steadfast support of other people along the way.

In your role as a nurse leader, you're in the cheering section, behind the concession stand, in the dugout with the clipboard—but not on the playing field. You exist to support others and organize systems so that, together, they can provide patients with the best possible care. In that capacity, it is imperative that you exhibit—and actually possess—a keen interest in others, not just be an interesting person yourself. Ask questions of your staff. Be curious about your colleagues' backstories—where they grew up, what they do in the organization, what their career trajectories have been, and so on. When others talk, absorb what they say: Be present, listen, observe, intuit—and *remember*.

Whether you are a budding nurse manager or a seasoned nurse executive, spend time in each of your areas of responsibility—as well as in departments and other areas of the organization that you and your team interface with regularly—to get a feel for the breadth of work roles throughout the organization. Devoting a full day to each shift, unit, or department can be a great way to gather perspective. Merely showing up and talking to a few people, on the other hand, just won't cut it.

If you have the chance to spend time on different shifts or in units and departments not directly under your supervision, ask questions of (and really listen to) those you meet. Find out what problems they face, what frustrations they experience, what disruptions and inefficiencies they deal with, and what ideas they have to make the place run smoother. Get to know these colleagues as people. Build relationships as best you can, finding out what it takes to admit a new patient, to navigate and organize the documentation in the electronic medical record, to gather supplies, to be in charge of a unit's nurses, and to navigate the communication among members of an interprofessional team. Understand what issues frontline workers encounter each day. Knowing what they do is a great way to be an authentic, effective leader.

Here are some tips for being interested in others and focusing less on yourself:

- **Learn to ask questions, and listen carefully and thoughtfully to the responses.** Ask people what's difficult about their jobs and what they find most rewarding. What processes and systems are ineffective or inefficient? What ideas do they have for improvements? Ask people what they care most about and what they find personally rewarding outside of work. Make sure you don't interrupt them while they're talking or turn the focus back on yourself.
- **When someone pays you a compliment, pay it backward.** After you say thank you, acknowledge that you had a lot of good help from many people along the way. Show that you're the kind of person who offers compliments and praise with regularity and ease, someone who recognizes that little is accomplished without the wisdom and contributions of others.
- **Replace fears about how you are being perceived with curiosity about others.** People often express worry about how they came across in an interview or while giving a presentation. Swap such thoughts with a determination to be inquisitive about others. If you are interested in others, there is no room left for you to worry about yourself.
- **Don't judge or get personal.** You will meet plenty of people who hold political views, religious beliefs, and values that are different from your own. Your job is not to judge or disapprove of others (unless their preferences and beliefs cause hostility, poor job performance, or fractiousness in your organization) but to be curious and interested in them as people. You are not out to preach or convert.

- **Celebrate important occasions.** Keep a master list of birthdays, and be diligent about sending cards or e-mails to staff to wish them well. Beyond birthdays, send notes of congratulations to colleagues who have received an honor or who have achieved a particular goal.
- **Write thank-you notes.** This one is important. In an era rife with technology, there is no substitute for a handwritten note of thanks. Keep a stash of basic thank-you notes in your desk. If someone invites you to a social event, gives you a gift, or does something that deserves a special thank-you, send a note of gratitude within 48 hours. If you're not able to handwrite the note, e-mail is the second-best option.
- **Exchange the pronouns *I, me,* and *my* with *we, us,* and *our.*** This puts the focus on teamwork and reinforces the group's efforts.
- **Keep your opinion to yourself unless it's related to the task at hand.** When asked for your opinion, frame it as something that "we" should do. That way, it seems less like an opinion and more like an accepted fact.
- **Learn and remember others' names.** Make it a habit. In meetings, if you don't know everyone sitting around the table, ask someone to help you with their names and positions, and write them down. Before meeting with people you have not met, look them up online and become familiar with their background.

It is said that true character is revealed by the way you treat those who can do nothing for you. When you are truly interested in others without regard for what they can offer you, you possess the foundation on which others' trust is built. Trust is necessary for honest and transparent communication, and many people can smell feigned interest from miles away. Always approach others as people with amazing stories rather than as people who are merely a work title or an organizational role to you.

EXERCISE 1

Complete an emotional and social intelligence survey instrument to identify areas for development. One such instrument is the Hay Group's Emotional and Social Competency Inventory survey, available at www.haygroup.com/leadershipandtalentondemand/our products/item_details.aspx?itemid=58&type=3&t=2.

EXERCISE 2

After identifying development areas in Exercise 1, attend a workshop, read books, ask your mentor for advice, and start unlearning old habits and learning new ones.

EXERCISE 3

Make it a habit to learn and remember names. When making rounds, learn at least one new name every time. Associate the person's name with a mnemonic, if needed.

RESOURCES

Forni, P. M. 2002. *Choosing Civility: The Twenty-Five Rules of Considerate Conduct.* New York: St. Martin's Press.

Goleman, D., R. Boyatzis, and A. McKee. 2013. *Primal Leadership: Unleashing the Power of Emotional Intelligence.* Boston: Harvard Business Review Press.

Use Mobile Devices and Social Media Wisely

Nurse leaders must adapt to cultural changes related to social media. There is a greater level of transparency and comfort with the sharing of personal information nowadays, especially among millennials who came of age with technology. The boundary between personal and professional life has blurred, and the result can spell disaster for healthcare organizations. With their openness to sharing, people risk inadvertently violating patient privacy laws. Managers need to recognize that what seems like common sense to them may not be obvious to some employees. Orientation should include specific guidelines about when and how patient information can be shared.

—Steve Thompson, PhD, RN, associate professor, Robins School of Business, University of Richmond, Virginia

STROLL ACROSS ANY university campus and you'll see students walking like zombies, texting or chatting on their smartphones, oblivious to the world around them. Such is our technological age—one of insularity riddled with self-absorption and a level of "connectivity" that actually breeds disconnect (and discontent). Our devotion to devices and social media offers a cautionary tale because this technology has, in fact, become hazardous to the health of interpersonal, face-to-face conversation. And in healthcare, as in other businesses, how you communicate person-to-person is what *really* matters.

Technology's big sell is the time savings it is supposed to provide. However, when used unwisely, these devices and platforms are actually time thieves. Sites such as Facebook, Twitter, Google+, Pinterest, and other social media channels consume vast amounts of time and energy that could be spent more productively. Even highly regarded networking sites such as LinkedIn, which can facilitate professional connections and collaborations, can suck you in if you spend too much time cultivating online relationships. The key is leveraging technology and social sites in moderation and knowing when to get out from behind your desk and away from your computer screen into the real world of real-time human interaction—not screen-to-screen but in the flesh.

Social media sites tempt people to cultivate robust online presences and to post information, pictures, and details about their personal lives that they might not otherwise offer in person—sometimes even the kind of information that may damage their professional image and reputation. Some sites provide electronic diary functionalities that may seem private but are accessible to nearly anyone. Even the comments you post on just about any website can be tracked back to you.

You should understand the risks associated with these sorts of activities so that you don't do something careless that can have lasting consequences. When you're searching for a job, you should know exactly what exists about you online, and if you don't like what you see, do something about it before it becomes a problem for you. Honestly, the best strategy to scrub your online image is to be sure it's squeaky clean from the get-go.

Some might perceive social media as professionally useful because they enable you to tap colleagues in a more personal way. So what's the difference between social and professional networking? The dividing line is blurry. But keeping your private and work lives distinct is important.

Like social media sites, omnipresent devices also seem to exert a gravitational pull toward networking. Smartphones and other mobile devices have become a necessity for many of us, but sometimes it's inappropriate to pull your phone out to check a message, answer a call, or see what your friends are up to on Instagram. Know when it's okay to use your device, and when it's not.

Here are some pointers to consider:

- **Turn off your phone during meetings, and stow it.** Unless you're expecting an urgent call, keep your phone out of sight so that you're not tempted to glance at it. Give the meeting and your colleagues the full attention they deserve.
- **Don't check messages during meetings.** Unless you are on call for emergencies, refrain from reading messages, typing, or texting.
- **If you must take a call, excuse yourself and step out of the room.** Begin your conversation once you've fully exited, not when you're halfway to the door. Keep it short and get back to the meeting.
- **Don't text and drive.** Many states have outlawed texting while driving. Messages can wait until you're home or in the office. If you do your very best thinking in the car, get a digital recorder to record your ideas or use a recording app on your phone to take hands-free notes.

Here are some social media considerations:

- **If you blog or use social media, make sure your posts don't contain anything dicey.** The same goes for any photos you share of your activities. Would you blush if your mom read or saw them? What about your colleagues? Would you mind if those pictures you posted were on the front page of the newspaper?

- **If you decide to use social media, take a close look at your profile.** Does it reflect what you want business contacts or prospective employers to see?
- **Feel free to post content about your job search, career, and professional interests.** Be clear about what you're looking for and what you're interested in, and "connect" with professional groups and "like" organizations that are in your career domain. If you participate in online discussions about professional topics, keep your comments clean and concise. No crazy rants, flip language, or questionable references.
- **Take a close look at the friends and groups you're connected with on social media.** Do they project the type of image you desire? Choose your friends wisely.
- **Never post someone else's image or information unless you have explicit permission to do so.** Otherwise, you could be held civilly or criminally liable. Also, never post information or photos that would violate your organization's network use policy or HIPAA (Health Insurance Portability and Accountability Act) privacy rules.
- **Never use your employer's logo on your personal site without permission.** If you share your views online, do so only as a private individual, not as a representative of your organization. If you feel angry or passionate about a subject, wait until you're calm and clearheaded before posting a reaction or statement.
- **If you're posting online, do so on your own time and on your own device.** Respect your employer's time and property. Don't use work time and equipment to participate in social media or online discussions.
- **Think before you post.** Nothing online is ever truly private.

As with diet, exercise, alcohol, and most of life, moderation is key when using technology and social media. Know when and why to use your devices. Excellent, high-quality work stems from clear-minded individuals who are able to process without distraction—and smartphones, Snapchat, and Instagram have nothing to do with it.

Many have learned hard, career-ending lessons when they failed to tame their online habits. So remember: If you do use a social or professional networking site, make sure it reflects your personal brand. Use it to highlight your education, experience, skills, and professional and community service. Let it show you as a thoughtful, perceptive human being. There isn't a lot of room for error, so it's best to be careful.

EXERCISE 1

Google yourself and see what comes up. Note what you were surprised by and what you'd have preferred to see at the top of the search results.

EXERCISE 2

Review your profiles on social media websites to be sure they reflect your personal brand. Ask an expert for advice.

RESOURCES

Nelson, R., I. Joos, and D. M. Wolf. 2012. *Social Media for Nurses: Educating Practitioners and Patients in a Networked World.* New York: Springer Publishing Company.

Thielst, C. B. 2014. *Applying Social Media Technologies in Healthcare Environments.* Chicago: Healthcare Information and Management Systems Society.

———. 2013. *Social Media in Healthcare: Connect, Communicate, Collaborate,* 2nd ed. Chicago: Health Administration Press.

Harness the Power of Mindfulness

Mindfulness is intentionally bringing awareness to the present-moment experience with openness and curiosity. Being mindful helps you to be in control and catch yourself before you react. When you're mindful, you can deliberately pause and step back for a moment to assess what's happening. You are vividly aware of your experience but aren't lost in it. With calm understanding, you can objectively consider the different potential outcomes of a situation. From this position of clarity, groundedness, and strength, you can thoughtfully speak, take action, or choose to do nothing.

—Susan Bauer-Wu, PhD, RN, FAAN, president, Mind and Life Institute, and adjunct professor, University of Virginia School of Nursing, Charlottesville

"ATTENTION," WROTE PHILOSOPHER Simone Weil, "is the rarest and purest form of generosity." But while the concept is simple enough, being *truly* present is incredibly hard. Our attentiveness is continually interrupted by a host of forces, especially electronic ones, that rob us from the moment. And although many routinely blame their devices, the real culprit is Americans' propensity to live in either the past or the future—not the present. We, and those around us—from our children to our spouses, from our colleagues to our clients—suffer as a result.

The most authentic leaders understand what it means to pay homage to the present. They practice paying attention and consciously notice new things—those with whom they come into contact, the connections that exist between others, the impact of the environment, how their bodies respond to particular situations, and how their minds interpret external stimuli. This practice, in its essence, is mindfulness—and it has the ability to shape one's destiny in powerful ways. Research has revealed that, if practiced effectively and often, mindfulness exerts a positive effect on health and well-being by redirecting stress and anxiety. Research has also shown that those who practice mindfulness are often more charismatic, creative, and innovative; are less judgmental; and tend to procrastinate less than those who don't practice mindfulness. Being mindful, not "mind-full," is simply a better way to live, to work, and to care.

Although a certain amount of life and work involves routine and repetition, *all* activities can be conducted mindfully—even eating and walking! If you operate continually (or even partially) on autopilot, you might miss something important—a nuance, a random but inspired idea or notion, or perhaps a connection to another that may lead to a better practice, a different way of thinking, or even a new job. It pays to pay attention.

When you live mindfully, serendipity often follows. Colleen, for example, had stayed in touch with her former professor and adviser after finishing school and moving out of state. She told him how frustrated and restless she was at her current job, mentioning that her dream had always been to teach. Her professor mulled over what she said. A few weeks later, at a conference, he found himself seated next to a faculty member at a university in Colleen's state. This individual happened to be serving on a search committee that was looking for someone with Colleen's experience. Ultimately, Colleen landed a job teaching undergraduate nursing students, and later, she pursued a doctoral degree. The point is, connections are made if people are open to them. In Colleen's case, a positive outcome resulted from paying attention, making connections, getting the right people together, and being open to serendipity.

More and more nurse leaders, hearing their staff complain about stress, are considering mindfulness practices as a resilience and retention strategy. Hospitals are increasingly offering regular meditation and yoga classes or have a special quiet room where clinicians and others can go to recalibrate after difficult interactions or emotional cases. Some hospital staff deliberately re-center themselves by taking a collective pause amid the chaos of an emergency department; others observe a moment of silence after a patient's death or after the stress of sharing a bad diagnosis. However mindfulness manifests itself in a healthcare organization, employees *at all levels* of the organization must be able to tap their inner resources. If the organization does not emphasize and provide access to such mindful practices and behavior, burnout and turnover—which are costly in terms of both financial and psychological bottom lines—can ensue. Healthcare is a rewarding field precisely because the work done matters so much. If healthcare workers have no way to boost their spirits and to deal effectively with adversity, their tenure will be short and their impact will ultimately be diminished.

There are many ways to practice mindfulness. In your practice, do what works best for you. Discipline and curiosity may be required, but the rewards are many. The following are a few techniques that are used for mindfulness:

- Meditation
- Centering prayer
- Yoga or Tai Chi
- Exercise
- Reflective writing

Whichever technique proves best, make it a habit. Put it on your schedule. Some nurses meditate with colleagues each week before breakfast. Others wake up at 5:00 a.m. and spend time writing in their journals. Still others take a solitary jog on deserted streets at sunrise. The point is to do the activity regularly.

Keep in mind that mindfulness isn't about checking something off a list; it's about making room to breathe and taking time to be still and present—nothing more. You don't have to become a New Age guru to do it—just a thoughtful person aiming to continue to be more so.

EXERCISE 1

Try a few of the exercises in Susan Bauer-Wu's *Leaves Falling Gently*, such as the following:

- Throughout the day, do mini–body scans by pausing physically and mentally and tuning in to how your body is feeling.
- Catch yourself when your mind creates unhelpful stories in response to what is happening in your body now or may happen in the future.

EXERCISE 2

Attend a yoga class or meditation group in your community. Learn loving-kindness meditation as a compassionate practice to bring a more generous spirit into your life.

RESOURCES

Bauer-Wu, S. 2011. *Leaves Falling Gently: Living Fully with Serious and Life-Limiting Illness Through Mindfulness, Compassion and Connectedness.* Oakland, CA: New Harbinger.

————. 2010. "Mindfulness Meditation." *Oncology* 24 (10 Suppl): 36–40.

Gelles, D. 2015. *Mindful Work: How Meditation Is Changing Business from the Inside Out*. New York: Houghton Mifflin Harcourt.

Howland, L. C., and S. Bauer-Wu. 2015. "The Mindful Nurse." *American Nurse Today* 10 (9): 12–13, 43.

Kabat-Zinn, J. 2005. *Coming to Our Senses: Healing Ourselves and the World Through Mindfulness*. New York: Hyperion.

Marturano, J. 2014. *Finding the Space to Lead: A Practical Guide to Mindful Leadership*. New York: Bloomsbury Press.

Salzberg, S. 2013. *Real Happiness at Work: Meditations for Accomplishment, Achievement, and Peace*. New York: Workman Publishing Company.

Develop a Personal Brand

Your reputation is created from your own principles, such as caring for others, honesty, collaboration, innovation, thoughtfulness, lightheartedness, and a touch of humor. In creating your personal brand, you must reflect honestly on who you are and what you stand for. This brand representing you and your style will resonate with others and will build personal and political capital that will carry you far in both good and challenging times.

—Garrett Chan, PhD, APRN, FAEN, FPCN, FNAP, FAAN, director of advanced practice, Stanford Health Care, Stanford, California

AS CHILDREN AND adolescents, we learned to fit in by having the latest clothes, shoes, hairstyles, toys, gadgets, and albums—tangibles that often felt like the sole pathway to status and acceptance. At these early points in life, being different felt like a deficit. What you realize as a grownup, however, is that standing out—and standing brave in your skin, with your values and morals intact—has power, merit, and immense worth. Being wholly yourself is always better than following paths determined by others; the best executives stand tall as who they are.

The transition from lemming to leader happens rather suddenly. When you enter the professional world, it becomes important to show how you're different from the pack. How you stand out and what values you bring or add to a place become your personal brand. These traits are critical to your success in any organization, and they have little to do with clothes, hairstyles, or gadgets and everything to do with who you really are and the unique assets, skills, and values you bring.

As children, we're taught a set of values and behaviors that reflect those values. Not everyone receives the same instructions at the outset, but by the time one moves into a position of managerial responsibility, one needs to have acquired basic manners. There is real economic value in cultivating your personal brand, so be sure you have the basics of politeness and good manners thoroughly covered.

Executive skills classes are traditionally part of every healthcare administration graduate student's coursework. This formal curricular content is rarely included in the graduate education of nurse leaders, however. These executive "grooming" sessions are particularly helpful to those who need to polish their manners to ensure a smooth transition into the workplace. It goes without saying that first impressions usually stick and that negative first impressions are nearly impossible to overturn. Many students and job seekers never quite recover from interview gaffes committed through lack of basic manners and social mores. Don't be one of them.

Managing the impression you make on others is a big part of working in any profession, and such impression management goes beyond your emotional and social intelligence. *How* you show the tenets of your personal code—your behaviors, actions, and responses—matters immensely. To have a successful personal brand you must first be open to seeing yourself wholly and critically, so monitor yourself and others' reactions to you closely and ask for feedback. The best way to know how others perceive you is to undergo a 360-degree performance evaluation, which involves input from your managers, peers, subordinates, and others.

But don't wait for others to tell you what personal gaps and skill deficits you have. You can boost the impression you make by absorbing lessons on business etiquette from books, by noticing how people you admire as professionals manage the impressions they make, and by asking others what they think are important attributes of leaders.

Here are a few tips to enhance your personal brand:

- **Know the rules of civility.** Start with a recent book on business etiquette. In our increasingly multicultural society, understanding appropriate manners for international settings is important, too. Social and business customs in one country may not apply in another. Learn the rules *before* you go abroad or interact with someone visiting from another country.
- **Get along.** Embrace feedback and criticism, and acknowledge and appreciate differences. You don't have to like everyone you work with, but you do have to get along. Always assume that others have positive intentions. Be humble and nice, and abandon any sense of entitlement. If you have an attitude, lose it.
- **Honor professional relationships.** Relationships take time to develop, so don't become too familiar with others in your work or profession when you first get to know them—particularly if they occupy a position of authority. Professional relationships may overlap with personal and social ones, but not necessarily. Some people choose to keep their work relationships strictly professional, and you must respect that choice. Proceed here with caution and care.
- **Be trustworthy.** If someone tells you something in confidence, always keep that confidence. You will cause irreparable harm to your credibility if you're deemed untrustworthy, and it takes only one mistake for this to happen.
- **Be grateful.** People rarely find success on their own. When someone pays you a compliment or gives you recognition, first say thank you, then share the praise by pointing to others' role in your success. If a colleague agrees to serve as a reference, send a thank-you note. Remember that if you

do something careless or stupid, it will reflect poorly on others who have vouched for you—an incentive to always do your best.

- **Run good meetings.** Have a purpose. Develop an agenda and stick to it. Distinguish between action items and items that are informational only. Agree on standards of behavior and process, and know how to disagree with others respectfully. If you're attending a colleague's meeting, arrive on time. Turn off your mobile device to be wholly present. Even if you're not feeling fully engaged, fake it as best you can because people will notice your demeanor. If you have to miss the meeting, be thoughtful enough to let the organizer know in advance.
- **Be engaged and engaging.** *Really* listen to what others are saying, and attempt to understand their reasons. Take in body language to gauge how the conversation is going. Consider what the others want, and be optimistic: Remind them that you're all seeking a positive outcome.
- **Learn.** Aim to broaden your horizons, and be willing to start on the ground floor to build a career. Be curious, and take an interest in what others do. Don't ever be too good for a task; everyone has to start somewhere.

Avoid succumbing to entitlement by keeping the following in mind:

- Having a first-class education or Ivy League affiliation doesn't entitle you to a good job or give you a particular advantage in the workplace.
- Being smart in school doesn't mean you're smart at everything. Listen, and show you can learn from others.
- Working hard doesn't mean you deserve an award, a promotion, or a pay raise.

- Just because someone is nice doesn't mean she will or should make exceptions to her standards or rules for you.
- Just because you were always at the top of your class doesn't mean you'll be the top performer in the workplace. Learning business takes time; employers care less that you know how to write a business plan and care more that you know how to execute it.
- Just because information is freely available online doesn't mean it's yours for the taking and doesn't require citation. Don't plagiarize.
- Just because you're married to your mobile device doesn't mean you should attend to it in the company of others. Others may think you're insensitive or rude and get the impression that your phone is more important than what (or who) is right in front of you.
- Just because you know someone doesn't mean that person owes you favors or special treatment. Social connections are wonderful—preserve them by not taking advantage.

So what works?

- Treat all people with kindness and respect, not just those who can be of use to you.
- Know your values and the behaviors consistent with those values.
- Don't take yourself too seriously. Be self-deprecating so others know that you don't always have to be right and that you can relax.
- Learn and practice mindfulness (see lesson 8). Be in the moment. Good things happen when you pay attention.
- Set your own boundaries, and respect those of others.
- Use proper grammar; avoid slang and profanity; and drop juvenile words such as *dude, like, you know, totally, awesome,* and *no problem* from your vocabulary.

- Don't drink excessively at business functions, whatever the function and regardless of what others are doing. Never have more than two alcoholic drinks at any business function.
- When someone asks you a question, don't respond by first saying they've asked a good question. If you need to buy time, a moment of silence before responding shows you're being thoughtful.
- Use the following liberally:
  - Please
  - Thank you
  - You're welcome
  - I was wrong
  - I'm sorry
  - What do you think?
- When you commit to follow up or to meet a deadline, do it. Being too busy is not an acceptable excuse.
- Excuses are not the same as apologies. Don't say why you didn't get something done or made a mistake. Say you're sorry and it won't happen again, and then make sure it doesn't.
- Avoid speaking ill of anyone behind their back (even if they deserve it).
- Learn what behaviors are expected in a healthy work environment (see lesson 45).
- Don't lose your temper. If you're about to, take a break.
- Be nice to everyone, and remember that anyone in the organization can be influential. It is not about the title.

EXERCISE 1

List three of your best traits, and write a one-sentence tagline that expresses your personal brand.

EXERCISE 2

Complete a Johari Window exercise (e.g., http://kevan.org/johari) to understand how others see you compared with how you see yourself.

RESOURCES

Pachter, B. 2013. *The Essentials of Business Etiquette: How to Greet, Eat, and Tweet Your Way to Success.* New York: McGraw-Hill.

Post, P., and P. Post. 2005. *Emily Post's The Etiquette Advantage in Business: Personal Skills for Professional Success,* 2nd ed. New York: William Morrow.

Write Well

Writing came easily to me, but writing well did not. I had to learn to be clear and concise and to engage with my intended reader. I found that when I invested the time to develop my thoughts carefully and to revise them as often as needed, I was more persuasive and answered most questions proactively. I have also found writing well to be a "power tool"—others can easily dismiss a verbal discussion, but if an issue is put in writing, they take the call to action seriously. Many important conversations can then begin.

—Marion E. Broome, PhD, RN, FAAN, dean and Ruby Wilson Professor of Nursing, School of Nursing, and vice chancellor for nursing affairs, Duke University, Durham, North Carolina

SOME SAY WRITTEN communication is fading into oblivion. Today, e-mail and text messages—often not employing proper grammar and drawing on a whole lexicon of abbreviations—make up the bulk of social and business correspondence. These formats don't offer the benefits of the handwritten note or formal business letter, however, nor have they adequately replaced it.

To write well, you have to know more than good grammar and punctuation. And whereas college courses required papers of a minimum length that rewarded wordiness, the business world demands the opposite. That one-page executive summary you're writing must elegantly contain all the contents of a ten-page essay. Executives have neither the time nor the attention span to read lengthy missives. They want to glean the main points and the recommended next steps. The art of concise writing is tricky and is only achieved through practice.

But tight, whittled-down language doesn't mean your writing has to be bland. Activate your words by avoiding forms of the verb *to be*. Use action words to convey meaning, and consider the effect of powerful adjectives. Use contractions occasionally to avoid sounding overly formal. Intersperse long sentences with short ones. Use bullets to break up long passages of text. And keep the tone as conversational as you can.

Following are some guidelines for specific types of business communications.

EXECUTIVE SUMMARIES

Think of an executive summary as your elevator speech: You've got only 90 to 120 seconds to convey your idea. Be succinct and engaging. Boil it down to no more than five main points. Use language that is easy to grasp without being too elementary. Don't obfuscate with fancy verbiage.

Note the difference between these two examples:

Version 1: Our internal quality improvement team is reading case studies. The studies are of three similar companies in the Mid-Atlantic with roughly equivalent numbers of patients, physicians, and nurses and operating budgets of at least $350 million annually. These medical centers are nationally ranked and have Magnet designation. With this research and by following their examples, we will figure out how to be a better, stronger, more profitable company.

Version 2: Case studies of similar institutions will help us chart a path toward Magnet designation and profitability. The best institutions have a profound emphasis on patients;

an exceptional devotion to safety and quality; and a focus on caregivers' compassion, resilience, and satisfaction.

THANK-YOU NOTES AND BUSINESS CORRESPONDENCE

Thank-you notes have the biggest impact when they are handwritten and sent immediately after the event (e.g., interview, meal, reference provided, professional favor). If mailing a thank-you note, make it more personal by using a stamp rather than putting it through your organization's postal meter.

If an administrative professional assists you with your business correspondence, proofread all letters before signing. A business letter should be like a framed piece of art: unmarred, centered, and straight on quality letterhead, with of course no errors in grammar or punctuation. The addressee's name, title, and address should be correctly spelled. If you receive someone's business card, mimic exactly the information given there.

Avoid fancy fonts or stationery that is anything other than strictly classic. Be consistent in using a standard typeface (e.g., Times New Roman or Arial) and font size (e.g., 12 point). Avoid mixing typefaces, excessive use of boldface, underlining, and italics. You may not want to rely solely on spell-checker because it can change proper names into incorrectly spelled ones. When you sign your name, do so in ink—in a contrasting color, if possible. A stamped or scanned signature implies you may not have been involved in the letter-writing process.

E-MAIL MESSAGES

Although e-mail has become the standard way to communicate at work, it can be inefficient and lead to unintended misinterpretation. Before you hit "send," consider doing the following:

- **Make sure that e-mail is the right communication tool for the job.** If you suspect that your e-mail will result in a lot of questions, a face-to-face meeting would be better.
- **Treat your e-mail as you would a written letter.** Just because it's an e-mail doesn't mean you can abandon capitalization, grammar, punctuation, and proper spacing. Don't type the content of your e-mail in the subject line as if it were a text message. Don't use texting abbreviations. Start your e-mail with a greeting, and close it with *Sincerely, Thank you, Do let me know,* or a similar phrase. Type your name at the end.
- **Get to the point.** Use the first three sentences of the e-mail to tell people what they need to know. If your colleagues are trying to schedule a meeting and asked about your availability, you do not need to go into detail about how busy you are; simply say when you're available.
- **Stick to one topic per message.** Communicate in a straight line without going off on tangents or other topics that distract from the main point.
- **Be clear about who should respond and by when.** You can even note the deadline in the subject line, along with two or three words summarizing the topic.
- **Use common sense when forwarding e-mails.** Don't make the recipient wade through the e-mail muck of a forwarded string. Start fresh, offering a sentence or two of context. Also, make sure the message you're forwarding does not contain sensitive information or snarky remarks.
- **Be transparent and inclusive.** If you are writing an e-mail that affects more than one person, include everyone on the same e-mail, addressing it to those who are critically involved and copying those who are tangentially involved.
- **Simplify your e-mail signature.** Be sure your electronic "business card" is simple and straightforward and doesn't

have your favorite quote, a lengthy description of your job title, or other unnecessary information.

- **Don't send anything you wouldn't want everyone in your company (or your mom) to read.** No office politics, snarky remarks, inappropriate content, or profanity.
- **Don't use emoticons.** Not now, not ever. Don't do it.

There are also certain guidelines to follow when *receiving* e-mails. The following are the most important:

- **Don't make assumptions about the sender's emotional state.** Hurried messages may seem to have an angry or upset tone that was not intended. If you receive such a message, pause. Switch tasks. Then reread the message later before responding.
- **Don't reply to confrontational messages.** E-mail silence offers you a position of poise and, frankly, of power. Respond either in person or by phone.
- **Ask for clarification in person.** Seeking clarity in person or over the phone, rather than by sending another e-mail, will save you time in the long run.
- **Keep organized.** Use color coding and folders to organize e-mails relating to the same issue. Block spam and junk mail, but check those folders periodically to ensure messages from colleagues and clients haven't gotten caught in your filter.
- **Don't respond to every message right away.** Designate regular periods during your workday to read and respond to e-mails. If you get in the habit of answering work-related e-mails during your off-hours or from home, your colleagues may expect that level of constant connectivity.
- **Set boundaries about personal e-mail.** Let your friends and family know when you check your personal e-mail. Set aside time to check and respond to personal e-mail before and after work hours.

EXERCISE 1

Write a one-page essay about any topic using no more than eight instances of the verb *to be*.

EXERCISE 2

Buy personalized note cards, and start practicing the art of writing notes.

RESOURCES

Connor, P. 2016. "Business Email." Colorado State University Writing@CSU. Accessed October 17. http://writing.colostate .edu/guides/documents/business_writing/business_email /index.cfm.

Mind Tools. 2016. "Communication Skills: Communicating Powerfully in Writing." Accessed October 17. www.mindtools.com /page8.html#writing.

Silverman, D. 2009. "4 Tips for Writing Better Email." *Harvard Business Review* Blog Network. Posted March 6. http://hbr .org/2009/03/4-tips-for-better-business-wri.

Speak Well

How do you recognize an excellent communicator? Whether addressing an audience of one or one thousand, an excellent communicator makes you feel like you're the only person in the room. Many communicators are knowledgeable and skilled—but only genuineness and humility will touch your heart and mind.

—Ramón Lavandero, RN, MA, MSN, FAAN,
senior strategic advisor and organizational historian,
American Association of Critical-Care Nurses, and
clinical associate professor, Yale University School of Nursing,
West Haven, Connecticut

SPEAKING WELL MEANS getting information across clearly, effectively, and—with luck—memorably. Those who speak well project confidence and authority. Whether you are addressing a group or speaking informally with someone one-on-one, *how* you speak says a lot about you.

Here are some simple questions to keep in mind when you're speaking, whatever the situation:

- **What is my aim?** Are you trying to inform, persuade, or both?
- **Who is my audience?** How much do they know about your subject? Why would they be interested in or care

about what you have to say? No one likes to listen to a speaker who talks down to the audience or speaks over their heads. If you know your audience, you can direct the content of your message appropriately.

- **What are the main points I want to make?** Rather than send out a tidal wave of information, you should give audience members three to five takeaways. Tell them what those points are at the beginning, explain each one, and then remind them of the points at the end.

- **What's my call to action?** What do you want people to do after they listen to you? You must invite them to support your idea, give you a job, join your club, or give you a raise. Don't assume they will infer—hypercommunicate (see lesson 26).

Get a solid sense well beforehand of the physical environment in which you'll be speaking. Consider how large the room is, how large your audience will likely be, and what equipment (e.g., microphone, podium, projector and screen) will be necessary. Will the audience have an opportunity to ask questions during or after your talk—and if so, how will they be heard? How long will your portion of the presentation last?

An oral presentation often follows a particular format, such as the following:

- **Start with an icebreaker.** This is your chance to harness the audience's attention. Good at jokes? Tell a funny story about yourself (never off-color) that segues into one of your main messages or themes. Some presenters ask for a show of hands in response to a particular question. The beginning is a critical time to introduce yourself—especially when speaking to large audiences—even if you believe you know everyone in the room. Explain what you do and why you're there.

The confidence with which you walk up to the podium, the way you smile, and how tall you stand are all part of your presentation.

- **Introduce and frame the topic.** Offer your audience a sense of how long you'll be talking, to help keep their attention.
- **Announce your outline.** Tell the audience which three to five takeaway points you'll focus on.
- **Name and number your central points.** "Now let us move on to point number one. . . ."
- **Flesh out each point with a real-life story or data that succinctly illustrate its significance.** Then pause to let the point soak in. Beware of tossing in too many numbers, however. Keep the data to a minimum and be sure they support your argument.
- **Break up your conclusion into four parts:** (1) Review your main points, (2) clarify the takeaway or action plan, (3) thank the audience for their time and attention, and (4) invite them to ask questions or make comments.

Inevitably, snags will arise before or during your presentation despite the best-laid plans—and, frankly, that's life. Your microphone may need a new battery or produce deafening interference, your slides may be out of focus, or your computer may crash. Your voice may give out. But as with everything in work and life, it's how you roll with it—and being able to do so, of course—that truly shows your mettle. *You* are the key ingredient in any presentation; the technology is, and should be, largely ancillary. What *you* have to share and how *you* compel others are most important.

How you handle complications says a lot about your leadership ability. If something goes awry, use a backup plan (so make sure you have one) and remain calm and good humored about whatever trouble has arisen. Never berate your support staff in front of others, whether verbally or with stares that kill. Even if you feel your stomach churning, your skin breaking out in perspiration, and your neck and face turning red and splotchy with embarrassment, do the best you can. Hold your head high and remember that you're on display. Do your best to act with confidence, even if you don't feel an inkling of it.

If problems arise, don't continually refer to them or apologize for them. If you truly need to stop your presentation to address an issue, call for a ten-minute break so that the audience can stretch their legs while you regroup. Don't make the audience sit there while you and your team try to fix what's broken. Move on as best you can.

Here are some tips for polishing your speech:

- **Never simply read what's on the screen.** Use bulleted note cards or cues instead. Your audience, unless they're in kindergarten, can already read.
- **Keep your gestures and posture natural and comfortable.** Stand firm on both feet, and avoid rocking, leaning, or slouching. If you're holding a microphone, know how far (usually six to eight inches) to hold it from your mouth.
- **Be aware of and avoid distracting behaviors.** Avoid jingling change in your pocket, touching your face, or playing with your hair.
- **Never curse.** Don't use even grade B swear words.
- **Be aware of not only what you say but *how* you say it.** This includes your volume, pitch, tone, stutter, and any stammering or use of filler words such as *like*, *you know*, and *um*. Finish sentences rather than stringing them together with *and* or *um*. Don't let your statements sound like questions by ending them with a rising pitch.
- **Evaluate your audience's response as you speak.** Make good eye contact, and watch for what they react to.
- **Always, *always* rehearse.** Practice in front of a mirror, with a recording device, in front of an honest friend,

or better yet, with a video camera. Self-evaluation is a powerful motivation for changing behaviors.

When you're speaking with difficult or rude people—or with those who interrupt—always remember that you can't go wrong with listening politely and then directly and firmly stating your point or counteropinion. Kill them with kindness, and keep your manner and tone professional.

Here are some tips for dealing with specific types of detractors:

- **Snipers:** When ignoring them doesn't work, confront them. Ask the sniper a question to clarify a nasty remark or off-handed comment.
- **Talkers:** Stop speaking and look directly at the talkers. When you capture their attention, smile, nod, and then continue.
- **Deadheads:** Look directly at them so that they're aware you've perceived their projected lack of investment or interest. Step toward them and ask them a question. Get them involved.
- **Know-it-alls:** Even if their comment makes you swell with annoyance, thank them for their input and continue. Avoid eye contact with them, and make a concerted effort to include others. If you're dealing with someone who Googles everything you say and corrects every error you make, defuse the situation by inviting that person to be the official fact checker.

Colloquial speech and informal jargon—such as *dude, no problem,* and *what's up?*—should be avoided. Conversely, be wary of peppering your speech with highfalutin words when simpler ones suffice. Avoid mumbling, talking too softly or too loudly, or speaking in a way that identifies you with a particular generation or social class.

When speaking to persuade, try a face-to-face approach first. Telephone communication is a second-best option, but e-mail is the least persuasive and should be used only as a last resort.

EXERCISE 1

Prepare a speech, and then present it in front of your webcam. Time yourself, and critique your presentation. Repeat the speech until you are comfortable with and confident in your delivery.

EXERCISE 2

Check out Toastmasters International (www.toastmasters.org), and attend one of their meetings.

RESOURCES

Diers, D. 2004. *Speaking of Nursing . . . Narratives of Practice, Research, Policy and the Profession.* Sudbury, MA: Jones & Bartlett Learning.

Gallo, C. 2014. *Talk Like TED: The 9 Public-Speaking Secrets of the World's Top Minds.* New York: St. Martin's Press.

Toastmasters International. 2016. "Public Speaking Tips." Accessed October 17. www.toastmasters.org/MainMenuCategories/Free Resources/NeedHelpGivingaSpeech.aspx.

Master Crucial Conversations

It is powerful beyond measure when nurses lend their voice to support other nurses, when nurses are the voice for patients and families, and when nurses ask questions about what does and does not matter. It matters that nurses speak up to relentlessly drive change—one small step or giant leap at a time.

—Clareen Wiencek, PhD, RN, ACNP, ACHPN,
associate professor and advanced practice program director,
University of Virginia School of Nursing, Charlottesville, and
president (2016–2017), American Association of Critical-Care Nurses

BEING AN EFFECTIVE nurse doesn't just mean advocating for patients and families; it also requires working with many different people and dealing with their unique personalities, habits, and work styles. It can be difficult to voice a contrasting point of view, to explain that someone's behavior or work style is negatively affecting teamwork, or to make the case for something you believe is in a patient's best interest.

However, while avoiding that difficult conversation with a colleague may be easier, remaining silent is dangerous because a patient may experience a substandard outcome as a result of your reticence. In fact, studies have shown that the majority of mistakes occur because of failures in interpersonal communications. Mastering crucial conversations is therefore essential to being a nurse leader.

The "Silence Kills" study, undertaken in 2005 by VitalSmarts and the American Association of Critical-Care Nurses, identified seven types of conversations that are especially difficult to have in healthcare yet are essential for healthcare professionals to master. The study showed that the quality of these crucial conversations is strongly correlated with medical errors, patient safety, quality of care, staff commitment, employee satisfaction, discretionary effort, and turnover.

The crucial concerns that are the most difficult to broach are grouped into the following seven categories:

1. **Broken rules:** Taking shortcuts that could be dangerous to patients or coworkers—for example, tearing the tip off the index finger of a glove to better feel a vein
2. **Mistakes:** Trouble following directions or showing poor clinical judgment when making assessments, triaging, diagnosing, suggesting treatment, or getting help—for example, prescribing a drug with the wrong timing, frequency, or dosage
3. **Lack of support:** Reluctance to help colleagues who exhibit symptoms of burnout or being impatient with them, refusing to answer their questions, or complaining when asked to do something—for example, ignoring or isolating a burned-out coworker
4. **Incompetence:** Concerns about the competency of another nurse, physician, or other clinical care provider— for example, a physician who has a reputation for using bad clinical judgment
5. **Poor teamwork:** Teammates who gossip, try to look good at the expense of others, or use divisive and splitting behaviors—for example, a nurse who declares what she will or will not do and refuses to chip in to help others

6. **Disrespect:** Workers who are condescending, insulting, or rude, demonstrated through verbal abuse in the form of yelling, shouting, swearing, or name-calling—for example, a physician or nurse colleague who becomes defensive and raises her voice when questioned

7. **Micromanagement:** People who abuse their authority by pulling rank, bullying, threatening, or forcing their point of view on others—for example, a charge nurse who pages other nurses to come to the desk just to tell them what to do or who says, "Do it because I say so!"

The "Silence Kills" study found that, instead of speaking up, most healthcare professionals stay silent when confronted with these crucial concerns. They delay taking action, withhold feedback, or go along with erroneous diagnoses rather than face potential abuse from a colleague. The pervasiveness of this pattern of disrespect is serious. Even more alarming, the study showed people had endured the disrespectful behavior for a year or more.

To break the code of silence, says Joseph Grenny—a business social scientist, cofounder of VitalSmarts, and coauthor of the *New York Times* best-selling book *Crucial Conversations: Tools for Talking When Stakes Are High*—four crucial conversations must take place:

1. **Leaders must speak up about the pervasiveness of crucial concerns.** Leaders cannot simply dismiss negative behaviors as the result of a few bad apples spoiling the workplace. To effect real change, leaders must acknowledge the frequency of the problem.

2. **Caregivers must directly confront disruptive behavior.** Leaders need to encourage and support all employees to speak up when they witness disrespectful behavior, mistakes, incompetence, or a violation of safety standards. If they don't, the organization risks delivering substandard patient care and creating an unhealthy work environment (see lesson 45).

3. **Nurse leaders must respond appropriately to escalations.** The "Silence Kills" study found that the avoidance of crucial conversations is not limited to peers confronting peers; managers also are reluctant to confront their direct reports, and nurse leaders may avoid addressing problems with physicians. Frontline staff will not want to engage in crucial conversations if they do not see their managers modeling that good behavior.

4. **Senior leaders must support any use of sanctions.** Leaders must back up nurse managers who take appropriate action to correct bad behavior. Senior leaders must be clear about what constitutes a code-of-conduct violation, disseminate these policies widely, and support employees who undertake the difficult work of engaging in crucial conversations.

So what's the best way to approach and engage in a crucial conversation? The book *Crucial Conversations: Tools for Talking When Stakes Are High* presents a seven-step model:

1. **Start with heart.** *How* you discuss a topic may be more important than *what* you discuss. Show empathy, acknowledge your positive intent, and maintain mutual respect. Although you cannot change others, you *can* change your response to others. Acknowledge and own your feelings, describing the other person's actions in a nonaccusatory way—for example, "When you do or say _____, I feel _____."

2. **Stay in dialogue.** Maintain a two-way exchange of information. Listen intently, repeat back what you heard, and ask for clarification when you don't understand.

3. **Make it safe.** People are more likely to open up when they feel safe. If someone exhibits defensive behavior—for

example, avoiding a topic or withdrawing—they may, in fact, be feeling unsafe.

4. **Don't get hooked by emotion.** Use the STATE tool: Share the facts, Tell your story, Ask for the other person's story, Talk tentatively, and Encourage testing to ensure a shared meaning.

5. **Agree on a mutual purpose.** Find a common ground you both can accept, such as, "We both want what's best for our patients."

6. **Separate the facts from the story.** The narrative of what happened can have many versions. What is fact, and what is opinion?

7. **Agree on a clear action plan.** Explore options for improving the situation.

Mastering crucial conversations can improve communication, ensure a healthy work environment, motivate others to achieve higher levels of success, and ultimately improve patient care. For these reasons and others, this competency is key for nurse leaders.

EXERCISE 1

Think about someone you work with who exhibits one of the seven crucial concerns. How will you go about engaging in a crucial conversation with that person?

EXERCISE 2

Engage in a role-playing exercise with a colleague, in which one of you is a bullying coworker and the other is the one being bullied. Next, reverse roles. What did you learn from the experience? How will it help you be better at responding to disruptive behavior?

RESOURCES

Clancy, C. 2014. *Critical Conversations in Healthcare: Scripts and Techniques for Effective Interprofessional and Patient Communication.* Indianapolis, IN: Sigma Theta Tau International.

Grenny, J. 2009. "Crucial Conversations: The Most Potent Force for Eliminating Disruptive Behavior." *Physician Executive Journal* 35 (6): 30–33.

Major, K., E. A. Abderrahman, and J. I. Sweeney. 2013. "'Crucial Conversations' in the Workplace: Offering Nurses a Framework for Discussing—and Resolving—Incidents of Lateral Violence." *American Journal of Nursing* 113 (4): 66–70.

Maxfield, D., J. Grenny, R. McMillan, K. Patterson, and A. Switzler. 2005. *Silence Kills: The Seven Crucial Conversations for Healthcare.* VitalSmarts and American Association of Critical-Care Nurses. Accessed July 24, 2016. www.aacn.org/WD/Practice/Docs/PublicPolicy/SilenceKills.pdf.

Patterson, K., J. Grenny, R. McMillan, and A. Switzler. 2012. *Crucial Conversations: Tools for Talking When Stakes Are High,* updated 2nd ed. New York: McGraw-Hill.

Stone, D., B. Patton, and S. Heen. 2010. *Difficult Conversations: How to Discuss What Matters Most.* New York: Penguin Books.

Conquer Negotiating

Life is full of negotiation. The goal of negotiation is by no means to win or lose. As part of the human experience, every negotiation enriches our lives. To reach a win–win solution, negotiating requires more than just knowledge and skill. One must get right to the purpose, drawing on courage, wisdom, patience, compromise, and humility.

—Lin Zhan, PhD, RN, FAAN, dean and professor, Loewenberg College of Nursing, University of Memphis, Tennessee

SKILLFUL NEGOTIATION CAN improve any organization's bottom line. It can result in fair and reasonable labor rates, optimal staffing patterns, and lower costs—not just the capital costs of equipment and construction but the service costs of physicians, consultants, and others too. Good negotiations can also improve revenues when working out reimbursement contracts.

Being a good negotiator contributes to your personal bottom line, too. When you are offered a new job, for example, negotiating prowess comes in handy in discussions related to salary, scope of responsibility, and deadlines for deliverables. If you can negotiate, you don't just take what you're handed; you assert yourself—and your wants and needs—firmly, eloquently, and always politely.

There's a popular idea that good negotiators are tough and hard-boiled and that their take-no-prisoners attitude and fearsome tactics are what really seals the deal. But railroading others isn't a best practice in *any* situation. The best negotiators listen, explain, and prepare. They are firm but kind. They don't act like jerks. They consider all possible directions a discussion might take before it happens. And they're ready for it.

Negotiations have a before, a during, and an after. During the prenegotiation phase, you'll decide the following:

- **Who will handle the negotiation:** Will a team represent your organization, or will a single person do so? The former has certain advantages: It forces preparation, allows team members to draw on one another's expertise, enhances listening skills, and provides an opportunity to caucus through focused discussion. A team also enhances interdisciplinary coordination because it allows you to assign someone to record what's said and by whom during negotiation.

- **What you need to accomplish:** Start with high (but reasonable) expectations, and stick to them. Success in negotiation is often linked to an ability to maintain high expectations while lowering the expectations of those you're negotiating with. But remember that goals must be realistic and supported by evidence. Aim high, but don't be unwilling to budge—know what outcome you would be willing to walk away with.

- **How to analyze your opponents' position:** First, scrutinize in advance their terms and conditions to fully understand what they're after. Then take it further: What are their unstated needs? Also consider what strategies and techniques have worked in the past and whom they will assemble to be part of their team.

- **What your strategy will be:** Decide how low you are willing to go in the event you need to settle. Just as you made sure your original goals are supported by facts and logic, make sure the low end of your expectations is realistic.

- **What the tone will be:** The tone you take is tricky because you don't want to be a pushover, but you don't want to be nasty, either. Assume a moderate stance, if you can. You're not there to win at all costs, particularly if you are dealing with employees whose loyalty and goodwill are critical (traits that can easily be marred in the process). However, you're not there to be dictated to, either. Find a middle ground that is firm but polite.
- **What additional items might be brought to bear:** Especially in cases of new hires and human resources negotiations, have a few things in your pocket that may seem negligible but can sweeten the deal if the other side is required to dramatically lower their expectations. For example, if the nurses' union is asking for a 10 percent raise and you know the budget won't allow more than 3 percent, consider other ways to fortify the deal. Free parking is one; more paid time off is another. Don't be afraid to be unconventional in your approach because it's not always the money that matters—the gesture, the listening, and the thoughtfulness often count just as much.

If you wish to be taken seriously, your opponent must perceive that you have bargaining power. Otherwise, you will lack an edge in the process. You might have it by position, reputation, knowledge, or deadlines, but you should stand tall in your authority as a negotiator. That said, no one individual or team should be authorized to fully commit the institution at the negotiation table. In your preparations, work with those who have ultimate authority—the CEO, the CFO, and other senior leaders—to know the ranges of give-and-take you plan to offer. Don't surprise them. All parties should know that it's not official until the boss signs on the dotted line.

The formal negotiation begins with an initial agreement about the meeting's agenda and procedures. Each side makes a presentation, and then a discussion follows. During this process, you should do the following:

- **Really listen to, understand, and acknowledge the opponents' position.** Let them talk first. Ask frank questions about their goals so that you can glean the acceptable ranges for settlement and ascertain which areas are flexible and which are less so. After you listen carefully, repeat what you heard and then ask them to confirm that your understanding is correct.
- **Present your arguments clearly and concisely.** When it's your turn to talk, don't go into impossible details that may suggest you're trying to obfuscate. Keep it clear, concise, and short. Make your best arguments at the beginning and end.
- **Identify areas where you and your opponent agree and where you disagree.** Do so periodically during the discussion. Use a respectful tone.
- **Assess what you'll concede in exchange for your opponent's concessions in other areas.** Be willing to give on issues that are less important to you but could be important to your opponent.
- **Keep it moving.** Don't utter the same points over and over without seeming to budge. Splitting the difference can sometimes work you out of the inertia.
- **Justify your concessions.** As you make offers, be sure your opponent understands your position and justification.
- **Keep your offers on a short leash.** When you concede, don't stray more than a few degrees from the numbers you decided on during your preparation. If you're discussing a raise, don't offer 3 percent and then agree to 10 percent. Too big a leap implies ineptitude and amateurishness. Make sure your concessions are within a decent range.

Once an agreement has been reached, document it. Prepare a memorandum of understanding (MOU), which will serve as the basis for the formal written contract. The MOU doesn't need to be anything fancy, but it should include the main agreed-on points. Don't sweat the minutiae at this point; those can be dealt with later. Have both parties sign the document.

As you negotiate, boost your own practice with the following time-tested negotiation skills—and take note of them when you see them in others:

- **Emphasize mutual interest.** Constantly remind your opponent that the objective is to achieve an agreement that is in the best possible interests of both parties.
- **Express statements as questions.** Rather than stating, "We should handle this by . . ." or "Your estimate of costs appears to be unsupported," you might instead ask, "How do you think we should handle this?" or "How do you support your estimate of costs?"
- **Keep quiet.** For many of us, silence is uncomfortable. Fight the urge to fill the void because it may encourage the opponent to talk and reveal more about his position.
- **Go second and start small.** Getting your opponent to make the first concession is usually advantageous. If you are the first to concede something, make it on an issue of minor importance.
- **Insist on tit for tat.** For each concession you make, get one from your opponent.
- **Make the other side seem unreasonable.** You could perhaps say, "We've made a number of concessions; now isn't it your turn?"
- **Don't be a slave to the deadline.** If you need more time, extend it.
- **Be funny and engaging.** A bit of humor takes some of the weight off the process, creates a feeling of cohesion and compatibility, and makes a solution seem all the more appealing—and more likely.

- **Rally your caucus.** Leave the room with your team to discuss a concession or settlement, or take a break to restore order if the conversation has become heated and tense.
- **Formally close the negotiation.** When you have reached agreement, strike while the iron's hot: Assert that it offers the best solution for both parties, and then move swiftly to prepare and sign the MOU.

Negotiating is something to practice and get comfortable with. Although formal tactics can give you some pointers and ideas, no single path exists through a negotiation process that can be maddening, frustrating, and lengthy—yet sometimes even satisfying. Just remember that negotiations about items both big and small can be mediated through two tactics: buying time and limiting your authority.

So when the surgeon stops you in the hallway and asks you for a new piece of equipment, be honest about the fact that you'll have to do some research. Say you'll discuss it with your boss and get back to her. *And then do it.*

EXERCISE 1

Complete a continuing education seminar on negotiating, such as the one offered by the American College of Healthcare Executives (www.ache.org/seminars/seminar.cfm?PC=NEGOT).

EXERCISE 2

Practice the techniques outlined in this lesson the next time you are negotiating for new equipment, additional staff, or similar requests. Reflect on the experience. What did you change about your approach? Did it change the outcome?

RESOURCE

Laubach, C. L. 2002. *Mastering the Negotiation Process: A Practical Guide for the Healthcare Executive.* Chicago: Health Administration Press.

Tackle Conflict

The provision of health services, particularly nursing care,
is fundamentally about relationships. The way we respond to conflict
in the clinical setting cannot be separated from the relational
nature of our work.

—Debra Gerardi, JD, MPH, RN, chief creative officer,
Emerging Healthcare Communities, LLC,
Half Moon Bay, California

CONFLICT IS AN inherent part of relating to other people. And for nurse leaders, addressing conflict is a daily part of the job of managing the delivery of nursing care. Conflict with colleagues, patients, patients' families, and even members of the community will erupt from time to time—it simply cannot be avoided.

However, conflict is not always bad. Engaging in conflict *effectively* can improve communication, de-escalate emotions, resolve differences, and enhance trust—all of which are essential to creating healthy work environments and ensuring safe patient care. It can also enhance work relationships, hone interpersonal skills, solidify interprofessional teams, and promote resilience.

So how do you reap the benefits of conflict? The following tips will help you approach conflict in ways that empower your staff, respect your patients, and move you toward resolutions that preserve the human connection:

- **Create connection with both yourself and others.** How you connect with others depends on how you connect with yourself. The more connected you are to your own needs, habits, and hot buttons, the more easily you'll be able to effectively engage in conflict with others. Therefore, reflect on your behaviors and strive to understand how you defend yourself when you feel threatened. Do you tend to withdraw, give in, or become more assertive? Being aware of how you "show up" in conflict is the first step toward connection. Connection with others happens when you are present and empathetic and when you listen to understand. You'll find this connection leads to the type of conversation that reveals the true source of the conflict and permits a collaborative approach to problem solving.
- **Know your conflict triggers and tendencies.** Figure out what provokes your anger or defensiveness. Is it feeling disrespected or excluded? The fear of failing or letting people down? This self-awareness will help you identify when you're being drawn into a conflict. Next, consider how you tend to respond. If your knee-jerk reaction is to quickly bark orders or take swift action, you may be missing an opportunity to fully understand the situation and connect with others. Knowing your conflict triggers and tendencies will help you see when you are contributing to the conflict rather than facilitating a resolution.
- **Truly listen.** Rather than listening for information that confirms what you already think is true, pay attention to what the other person's real concerns are. Don't interrupt to ask questions, and acknowledge what matters to the other person by repeating back what you've heard. Truly listening demonstrates respect and often reveals the true source of the conflict—ensuring you won't waste time solving the wrong problem.

- **Be curious.** As a nurse leader, you have been trained to ask questions that gather information to help you make decisions. However, effective conflict engagement requires you to ask questions from a place of curiosity rather than from a desire to confirm your preferred solution. For example, asking "Why did you approach the situation *that* way?" implies judgment and may distance you from the other person. But asking "What impact has this situation had on you?" shows you are curious, engages the other person, and elicits information that will help move the situation forward.

- **Seek common ground.** In healthcare, we all want what's best for the patient: safe, effective care. Acknowledging this common ground will help uncover solutions to conflicts by aligning stakeholders, reducing defensiveness, and providing hope. Start by saying, "We clearly all want what's best for the patient, and everyone has some ideas of what that might look like. Let's begin there."

- **Remember your values.** Nurses have a duty to "do no harm." But in the heat of conflict, that code of ethics may be easily forgotten. In defending ourselves, we may harm others by diminishing them or, worse, behaving in a way that disrespects their fundamental human needs. By engaging in conflict in a professional and ethical manner that honors your foundational values, you can solve problems while leaving your integrity intact. You became a nurse to help others heal, and remaining mindful of your values—even in conflict—is essential to that work.

- **Consider patterns, not events.** Healthcare organizations are complex systems with many moving parts. No one can know about or control all the interdependent pieces, nor can one respond to every conflict that emerges from the intertwined relationships. Instead, learn to look for and address behavioral patterns. Bullying, for example, is rarely a one-time event; it's usually a symptom of a larger dynamic in which ineffective coping behaviors are dominating and poisoning the workplace. Address these patterns of conflict by engaging the individuals involved in conversations that make them aware of their behaviors and the effect the behaviors are having on the organization.

- **Solve the problem together.** A nurse leader may feel responsible for single-handedly resolving all issues all the time. Not only is this unrealistic, but it also disempowers others and prevents them from learning. Instead, engage those who are generating the conflict and involve them in resolving it. Ask them questions, invite their insights, and seek their help. Such collaboration holds employees accountable for disputes and teaches them how to engage, expanding their skills and demonstrating respect for their capacity to resolve differences on their own.

- **Create a process.** Resolving conflict in a clinical work environment takes more than just a chat. The presence of multiple stakeholders, complex issues, and varying power dynamics requires collaborative processes that encourage direct conversation among the various participants. Examples of such processes are open listening sessions, moderated dialogues, facilitated meetings, coaching sessions, and informal mediations. Consider how you can design structures for conversations in which people feel able to speak up; to acknowledge their emotions; and to air their concerns without fear of judgment, attack, or retaliation. Pave the way for a resolution that is humane and healing.

- **Stay engaged.** The desire to avoid conflict is a powerful barrier to engagement and may be the biggest cause of chronic conflict patterns. Avoidance can manifest in many ways; moving to solutions too quickly, skipping meetings, ignoring e-mails, pretending to be confused, and abusing power are just a few examples. Deciding when to engage is a fundamental conflict skill. Remaining engaged over time, especially with complex situations, requires viewing conflict as an opportunity for learning and for optimizing the work environment. Nurse leaders must take a broad perspective of the situation and adopt a strategic approach.

- **Choose compassion.** Nursing leadership can be simultaneously daunting and meaningful. Addressing conflict on a regular basis takes a toll on even the best leaders. Self-care and self-compassion are important components in effective conflict engagement and will help you stay grounded and rejuvenated. Resolving conflict from a place of compassion will align your work with the foundation of nursing practice and promote healing.

Endless sources of conflict exist in every organization. But true leaders manage a way out of the morass and allow everyone involved to get a little something they want while not acquiescing entirely to any one person.

As a nurse leader, you will experience many conflicts during your career. Do not try to avoid them. Rather, work hard to make sure conflict does not become personal, and seek solutions that will be permanent and systemic. The way you resolve conflict will be key to your success as a nursing leader. Ongoing conflict can sap an organization of its energy—energy that should be focused on carrying out its mission.

EXERCISE 1

Practice listening to what others are arguing about without interrupting anyone—not once. Think about what they are saying and why they are saying it. Have they mentioned a possible solution to the conflict?

EXERCISE 2

Read one book and one article on conflict management. Ask experienced managers whom you respect how they resolve conflict. Learn from their success stories.

RESOURCES

Fisher, R., W. L. Ury, and B. Patton. 2011. *Getting to Yes: Negotiating Agreement Without Giving In*, revised ed. New York: Penguin Books.

Mangold, K., and C. J. Hahn. 2014. *Confidence in Conflict for Everyday Life: Proven Strategies for Conflict Resolution and Communicating Under Pressure*. Milwaukee, WI: Truths Publishing.

Scott, C., and D. Gerardi. 2011. "A Strategic Approach for Managing Conflict in Hospitals: Responding to the Joint Commission Leadership Standard—Part 1." *Joint Commission Journal of Quality and Patient Safety* 37 (2): 59–69.

———. 2011. "A Strategic Approach for Managing Conflict in Hospitals: Responding to the Joint Commission Leadership Standard—Part 2." *Joint Commission Journal of Quality and Patient Safety* 37 (2): 70–80.

Commit to Integrity and Ethical Behavior

We frequently think of ethics and integrity as though they were something outside of us, almost imposed on us, when in reality they mean living out the best of who we are. They mean recognizing who we are called to be, and living out that call. When we are true to ourselves and live out of our core, others see that truth in us and trust us. We create an environment of trust where our words and behaviors are one. This environment of trust draws others to the safety of being truthful and honest, which magnifies in the environment of trust.

—Sister Patricia Eck, CBS, congregation leader,
Congregation of Bon Secours, Marriottsville, Maryland

HEALTHCARE IS UNLIKE any other profession and is a special domain for a host of reasons. Because its core operation depends on ethical behavior and integrity without interruption or fail, *how* employees conduct themselves is consistently of paramount importance—as is how the organization governs itself when things or people go awry.

All nurses must familiarize themselves with and be accountable to the *Code of Ethics for Nurses* of the American Nurses Association. The *Code of Ethics for Nurses* contains standards of behaviors to guide nurses' professional relationships, including those with colleagues, patients, other stakeholders, the external community, and society as a whole. It also outlines standards of ethical behavior to guide individuals' conduct, particularly when that conduct directly relates to the role and identity of the nurse. Nurse executives are also guided by the *Code of Ethics* of the American College of Healthcare Executives.

Of course, ethics and integrity were part of your life well before you moved into a formal leadership position. Nurtured by your family, friends, and teachers, your own personal code of ethics guided you through early life, informing your education, first jobs, and relationships. You have had a sense of right and wrong from childhood. But for working adults, issues are rarely as black and white as they are for kids. In life in general, and in the world of healthcare in particular, there can be many shades of gray.

In your work, as in life, there will be times when your personal code of ethics feels violated by another's actions. If this happens repeatedly, and without resolution or reconciliation, you're prone to what nurse researchers Ann Hamric and Elizabeth Epstein call the *crescendo effect*—a cycle of moral distress that you feel powerless to change. This cycle leads to burnout; disengagement; and ultimately physical, emotional, or psychological health issues. Some people even leave their profession altogether because of it.

Over the course of decades of teaching leadership classes, we've asked students of all ages and from all backgrounds what they believe the most important leadership traits to be. Without exception, integrity is among the first mentioned. But although everyone seems to agree that integrity is a critical character trait, there is little consensus about what constitutes integrity or the specific behaviors that manifest it. Merriam-Webster defines *integrity* as "the quality of being honest and fair" and "the state of being complete or whole," but integrity goes a lot deeper than that.

So what can you do to ensure integrity and a spotless ethical character? Have an inner compass, and follow it. Also keep the following advice in mind:

- **Be authentic.** If you take the time to connect with people in real ways, it will lead to trust.
- **Tell the truth.** Tell it as you honestly see it, and base it on reality. Also, say what you mean: Let your yes mean yes, and your no mean no.
- **Hear people out.** Listen and synthesize what people tell you. Listening intently, particularly when it really matters, is a key ingredient in authenticity.
- **Keep your promises.** Do what you say you will do. Do it on time and in the manner promised. And keep your work quality consistently high—don't offer half-baked responses or shoddy work.
- **Embrace and deal with the negatives.** Admit up front when you are at fault, and if you owe someone an apology, offer it without hesitation. Listen to those who have experienced fallout from your decision making. Then assume a "where do we go from here?" stance, if appropriate.
- **Commit to growth and transformation.** Be a visionary, big-picture type, but never lose sight of those whom you depend on to get you there. In other words, see the big picture but pay attention to details and people.
- **Keep it classy.** In conflicts, don't hit below the belt, even if you feel like it. Consistently take the high road. Always keep your professional cool.
- **Acknowledge and disclose conflicts of interest.** Never accept gifts from a customer or vendor if doing so puts you in a compromising position. If it feels even slightly wrong, it is. Don't do it.
- **Behave.** Don't do anything that you wouldn't want your mother (or your boss) to read about on the front page of the newspaper.
- **Sync up.** Be sure your personal values align with the values of your organization.

- **Know the boundaries of your personal code of ethics.** Know where you'll compromise and where you'll draw your line in the sand.
- **Don't cave in to peer pressure.** You know right from wrong. Don't feel pressured to give in to what you see others saying or doing if you think it's wrong.

EXERCISE 1

Write down what you consider to be your five most important personal values.

EXERCISE 2

Write a personal code of ethics—a description of behaviors that reflect your values.

RESOURCES

American College of Healthcare Executives. 2016. *Code of Ethics.* Amended November 14. www.ache.org/abt_ache/code.cfm.

American Nurses Association. 2015. *Code of Ethics of Nurses with Interpretive Statements*. Published January. http://nursingworld.org/codeofethics.

Cloud, H. 2006. *Integrity: The Courage to Meet the Demands of Reality.* New York: HarperCollins.

Epstein, E. G., and S. Delgado. 2010. "Understanding and Addressing Moral Distress." *Online Journal of Issues in Nursing* 15 (3): Manuscript 1. doi:10.3912/OJIN.Vol15No03Man01.

Filerman, G. L., A. E. Mills, and P. M. Schyve. 2013. *Managerial Ethics in Healthcare: A New Perspective*. Chicago: Health Administration Press.

Perry, F. 2013. *The Tracks We Leave: Ethics and Management Dilemmas in Healthcare*, 2nd ed. Chicago: Health Administration Press.

Look the Part

Make sure the first impression you make is a positive, lasting one. Even before you say hello and shake someone's hand, that person has already formed perceptions about your level of professionalism and confidence. The little things make all the difference, and professional appearance does matter. People will appreciate how much you know once they know how much you care, and that starts with the way you look and carry yourself. Make your first impression pop!

—Janie Heath, PhD, APRN-BC, FAAN,
dean and Warwick Professor of Nursing,
University of Kentucky College of Nursing, Lexington

IN NURSING, SOME have debated the type of dress that is most appropriate as one moves up the ladder of progressively responsible management positions. Some nurses believe business attire should be the standard apparel, while others think nurse managers should wear scrubs to identify with the staff nurses. Ultimately, the decision depends on organizational culture. Take note of how other successful nursing leaders in your organization dress, and follow their example. You can't go wrong by wearing business attire, but keep some clean scrubs and a pair of clogs in your office in case you are called on to help in a staffing emergency.

In college or graduate school, you might have been lax on the hair stylist appointments, lived in scrubs, or went without shampooing your hair during exam week by donning a hoodie or a baseball cap. One good interview suit, a couple of dressy outfits, and a few pairs of shoes were sufficient. With full-time professional employment, however, comes the need to consider and invest in a professional appearance. Now you need to wear business attire five days a week, with time built in to drop off and retrieve outfits at the dry cleaners. Although it doesn't matter exactly how many clothes you have, you should look the part each and every day. And that means looking like you care.

Many organizations have experienced great change in just a generation insofar as attire is concerned. Women no longer always wear dresses and heels, and men don't always don ties and sport coats. Even the leaders of large, well-regarded, multimillion-dollar organizations may lack a top-to-bottom formality in dress. Yet, leaders always keep their outfits classic and simple. You can't go wrong with that.

But dressing well means more than having an expensive suit or Italian-made slingbacks. Just as your mother told you, a great deal of beauty comes from within. If you dress well; pay attention to your grooming; cultivate a warm smile; and come across as friendly, articulate, and caring, you will be good-looking on many fronts. Looks are all in the smile and the eyes. Smiles that light up a room are magnetic and powerful. Eyes that twinkle show you are full of life—and good ideas.

Beyond clothes are the other items: your posture, your stride, your handshake, and even how you laugh. When you walk into a room, stand erect with your head held high. Look around at others and smile. Your handshake should be firm and confident. This is not the time to slouch, slump, or look scruffy. It's not the time to fidget nervously, bite your nails, swagger, chew gum, or twirl your hair. Own the skin you're in, even if you feel like you're faking it. Confidence is 100 percent appealing, even if you feel only 35 percent self-assured.

Here are some additional recommendations and considerations from the business field for maximizing your professional appearance:

- For both men and women:
  - Wear clothes that are clean, pressed, and well tailored—nothing too tight, too short, too risqué, or too frilly.
  - Wear cologne or perfume sparingly, if at all.
  - Keep your hands clean and your nails well manicured.
  - Keep your hair clean and well styled.
  - Wear shoes that are polished and unscuffed.
  - Make sure leathers match (e.g., shoes and belt).
  - Cover tattoos and piercings (other than women's earrings).
  - Keep jewelry to a minimum.
  - Insider tip: Take your dress cues from other, more senior administrators. Follow their degree of formality, considering regional and geographic variances in attire as well as rules for casual wear (e.g., sandals, jeans on Friday). Some dress code rules are unwritten but are nonetheless present in the organization's culture.
  - Insider tip: Dress as though it's a special occasion (which it is—every day). Convey through dress that you care and that you're confident and in control.
- For men:
  - Shave every day or keep facial hair neatly trimmed (including ears, nose, and eyebrows).
  - Use collar stays for dress shirts to avoid the flyaway look.
  - Wear suits with classic, conservative colors such as navy blue, brown, or gray. Reserve black suits for formal occasions, such as weddings and funerals.
  - Choose stylish ties that hang low enough to touch the top of your belt buckle.
  - Wear lace-up shoes with suits, slip-ons or loafers with sport coats and dress pants.
  - Match socks with the color of your suit pants.

- Avoid button-down-collared shirts, khakis, and penny loafers, which are more collegiate than business professional.
- Have pant cuffs tailored so that they fall lightly over your shoes and cover your socks when standing.
- Ensure shirt cuffs extend a half inch beyond the sleeve of your suit jacket.
- Insider tip: Keep a spare tie, sport coat, and hygiene products (e.g., toothbrush, deodorant) in the office.
- For women:
  - Keep necklines conservative.
  - Avoid sheer or lacy fabrics.
  - Make sure your skirt length is conservative but stylish.
  - Keep makeup subtle and natural looking.
  - Wear sleeveless tops only in the height of summer and with a modest skirt or pants.
  - Choose shoes with heels that are no higher than 1 to 2 inches; wear closed-toe shoes unless it's the height of summer.
  - Keep jewelry and accessories to a minimum (e.g., a purse), and avoid anything large, dangling, or noisy.
  - Insider tip: Dress up conservative apparel with bright colors or bold accessories (e.g., a brightly colored scarf or chunky necklace with a dark suit).

Good grooming and a professional appearance send a message that you are poised and confident and that you understand the unwritten rules of how to conduct and present yourself in the workplace. Although you may not have the budget early in your career to completely revamp your wardrobe, you can still take a strategic approach and buy quality clothes that will be a smart long-term investment. For men or women, a well-made, nicely fitting navy suit (suit coat and pants or pencil skirt) is a great place to start. From there, you can begin to take over the world—and accessorize your way as you move up the career ladder.

EXERCISE 1

Take an inventory of your clothes and shoes. Have you worn them in the past year? Are they out of style? Develop a plan to purge clothes that no longer work for you, and budget for replacements. When suits start to look shiny, shirt cuffs fray, ties look tired, and socks have worn areas where the shoes rub, it is time to give them up.

EXERCISE 2

Identify someone you consider to be a stylish and professional dresser, and ask for advice about how to develop a wardrobe. He or she may also be able to refer you to a salesperson who can advise you on a wardrobe that fits your budget.

RESOURCES

Baumgartner, J. 2012. *You Are What You Wear: What Your Clothes Reveal About You.* Boston: Da Capo Lifelong Books.

Dye, C. F. 1993. *Protocols for Health Care Executive Behavior: A Factor for Success.* Chicago: Health Administration Press.

Gross, K. J., and J. Stone. 2002. *Dress Smart Men: Wardrobes That Win in the New Workplace.* New York: Chic Simple.

————. 2002. *Dress Smart Women: Wardrobes That Win in the New Workplace.* New York: Chic Simple.

LESSON 17

Anticipate and Prepare

Every day in the life of a chief nursing officer is different from the day before, because the hospital work environment is dynamic and ever changing. At Virginia Tech, April 16, 2007, was a day like no other. The mass shooting on campus that day forever changed my appreciation for the role hospital leaders play in response and recovery efforts following mass-casualty emergencies. We learned many lessons during this event, in particular the importance of including all stakeholders in the development of emergency plans and involving them in regular drills that are conducted so carefully they feel "real." Prior to the Virginia Tech shooting, the community of Blacksburg, Virginia—including law enforcement agencies, local volunteer rescue personnel, and hospital providers—had drilled regularly and established clear communication channels for community emergencies. Lives were saved as a result of this planning.

An additional lesson learned was the prolonged and devastating effect this event had on emergency responders and hospital caregivers. Every hospital executive must place a priority on providing emotional and psychological support, both immediately and ongoing for days and even months following the response, because the post-traumatic recovery phase of individual caregivers varies and may be prolonged. Finally, hospital leaders must recognize that the hospital becomes a sanctuary for the community in disaster situations, and they must develop plans for accommodating the multitudes who will seek shelter and support.

—Loressa Cole, DNP, MBA, RN, FACHE, NEA-BC,
chief officer/executive vice president,
American Nurses Credentialing Center,
Silver Spring, Maryland

THE SCOUT MOTTO is "be prepared." Few things are more troubling than people who show up to critical conversations like blank slates—needing to be brought up to speed, asking questions they should have considered long ago, and attempting late in the game to bring their understanding up to par. Even if unintentional, such behavior not only is rude but also drains morale and the bottom line. It withers confidence and goodwill. And it makes the time waster an object of frustration and, worse, of ridicule.

Not being a time waster means you're prepared for each and every conversation, meeting, task, and project. You've considered in advance what the issues are and how you'll face them. Even in the early days of determining a solution, you've got a few ideas in your head to share and offer direction, and you're well aware of what the challenges are. In short, you've cared enough to think through issues in advance so that you're fresh and ready to offer pathways toward a solution.

If you prepare for a test, a good grade usually follows. But if you wing it or hack and fake your way through, the result is usually panic and a failing mark. In healthcare, as elsewhere, it's critical that you learn to anticipate and prepare. Don't waste people's time—*be prepared*. It's really that simple.

For meetings, do the following:

- **Arrive early and ready to focus on the issue at hand.** Turn off your electronics, and give your colleagues your undivided attention.
- **Prepare.** Imagine ahead of time the questions you'll be asked that are in your domain. Know and anticipate problems you might encounter along the way that touch your area of responsibility.
- **Huddle with your team.** Convene with close staff prior to a big meeting to discuss what's on the agenda, the questions you might be asked, and the solutions you plan to present. Several heads are often better than one.

- **Follow up.** If you're asked a question you can't answer, find the answer afterward and promptly report back.

Each day, try to do the following:

- **Plan longer-term.** Prepare for the next day's activities at the end of each day, and anticipate the next five days by outlining in your mind or on paper what generally will need to be discussed, accomplished, and considered. If you're working on a long-range project—for example, an initiative that will launch six months or a year from now—map out in advance how you'll get there and what tasks will need to be completed along the way. Put electronic reminders to yourself on your calendar to prompt progress toward your goal.
- **Feel people out.** Take time to understand what your team thinks about the issues and projects before them, and know the decision maker's perspective, too. Early discussions will help you understand possible solutions and sense when a consensus has been reached. The most successful leaders have a good idea of how a discussion or vote will go before it takes place. If a key individual has strong feelings or a big stake in an issue, consider his view before raising the topic at a meeting.
- **Be of service.** Know what your team is working on, and consider ways you can help, no matter how small. Making copies, getting water, taking coats—small things can really make a difference.
- **Don't surprise anyone.** If you have bad news to share, inform all stakeholders. Tell your boss, and discuss how you'll inform others in a calm, solution-oriented way. Without minimizing the bad news, keep your comments factual and then move quickly to solutions.

- **Prepare for the unexpected, and don't be derailed by it.**
  It's a truism that in life you can't prepare for everything.
  Having a good understanding of your organization's
  culture and goals will help you when the unexpected
  happens. If you've overlooked something or made an
  error, own it and say how you'll remedy it—for example,
  "I didn't speak with Dr. Nice about the project, but I will
  reach out to get her input when I return to my desk."
- **Review how well you prepared at the end of each day.**
  Learn from mistakes and do better tomorrow.

If you're able to cultivate a reputation as someone who prepares
for and anticipates problems and their solutions, you'll have a leg
up on many in your organization who will consider you a go-to.
Flying by the seat of your pants through any task or issue is never
advisable, and preparation and anticipation will help make you a
remarkable and effective nurse leader.

EXERCISE 1

Make an inventory of all of your areas of responsibility that require
anticipatory and emergency preparedness planning. Are your plans
and drills up to date? Are you ready for a mass-casualty event or
other threat to your organization?

EXERCISE 2

Make a list of priorities for yourself, your boss, and your organization
over the next year. What small tasks can you omit from your daily
routine that will allow you to focus on more important priorities?

RESOURCES

Babauta, L. 2009. *Zen Habits: Handbook for Life*. CreateSpace Independent Publishing Platform.

Cartwright, T., and Center for Creative Leadership. 2007. *Setting Priorities: Personal Values, Organizational Results*. San Francisco: Pfeiffer.

LESSON 18

Build Resilience

There is nothing magical about building resilience. It involves practicing a series of learned behaviors: getting enough sleep, taking time to exercise, cultivating a sense of humor, expecting regular failures and treating them as course corrections, and understanding that you cannot be strategic if you're wallowing in self-pity. Not only are these skills essential for the caregiver to develop, but they are also the building blocks we need to teach those persons in our care.

—Angela Barron McBride, PhD, RN, FAAN,
distinguished professor and university dean emerita,
Indiana University School of Nursing, Indianapolis

WE ALL LEAD busy personal and professional lives, with stress swirling all around us. Nowadays, a certain amount of chaos, intense activity, and drama must be taken for granted. But it's *how* we handle and defuse stress—and what inner resources we tap in the process—that reveals our true mettle and is a real key to success.

It's fascinating to observe how some who have faced tremendous hardships and tragedy are able to move beyond them, turning negatives into opportunities for growth and change. On the flip side, others never seem to fully recover from traumas such as divorce, the death of a loved one, or being fired. What accounts for the difference? How do some people harness resilience and perspective whereas others cannot?

A story to illustrate: A nursing student encountered one of his first patients, a man named Bill, who had been diagnosed with sarcoidosis—a chronic, incurable disease. Bill had lived with the disease for a long time and periodically spent time in hospitals for what he called "tune-ups." When answering questions about his illness and how it had changed his life, Bill was resolute and open: He found strength in faith and prayer and was grateful for each day, for being able to spend time with his large family, and for the opportunities his remaining days would bring. These were not just the canned utterances of a man who had heard or read such sentiments before; they were qualities evident in his engagement in the present, in his ability to accept and move beyond his tragedy with an uncanny level of beauty and grace. Few would deny that Bill had mastered the ability to face his illness head-on, find meaning in it, and do the best he could with the time he had to live. After he died, Bill's message of resilience never left the student.

Resilience really is about choosing the path of hardiness rather than the one of festering stress. Those who live with high levels of stress and unhappiness often give away their power to reframe the situation and harness control over it. They wait for others to change, or they focus on a situation or an event that they cannot control to the near exclusion of everything else. They're dissatisfied, disappointed, and disillusioned, and their bodies, minds, and families suffer as a result. They're more victims than victors.

These people come at a cost. When others attempt to reframe what's upsetting them and offer suggestions to ease the stress, these individuals resist. Their negativity bleeds out, sucking away the energy and momentum of others—even of whole organizations. They've missed the message that *at any point in life* resilience can actually be learned and followed.

Organizations can be resilient—or not—as well. Companies that are able to face reality, to turn negatives into opportunities, and to nimbly regroup and resource a turnaround will always have the competitive edge. In contrast, organizations that deny problems, shy away from risk, and never make plans to deal with future potential hardships will ultimately suffer and die. In the dynamic, fast-changing world of healthcare, it's critical to be the former.

Being resilient begins with harnessing a positive attitude and practice, being willing to thoughtfully change, and being ready to move and find solutions without getting stuck in the quicksand of inertia. Some healthcare organizations even practice *resilience engineering*, a new approach to patient quality and safety that involves sustaining required operations under expected and unexpected conditions. Such exercises truly show an organization's—and a team's—ability to think on its feet through a crisis. Such activities might even turn stressed-out organizations into resilient ones.

Resilient practices such as meditation, yoga, reflective writing, deep breathing, and even physical exercise make for happier, stronger, and more centered clinicians. These contemplative practices can form a foundation for human flourishing and bring out the best in us.

So how do you bring resilience into your personal life and infuse it in your organization?

- **Consider a contemplative practice.** Take time to pause and thoughtfully consider what will serve you to become your best self.
- **Face reality but sustain optimism.** In difficult situations, rose-colored glasses may make the situation worse. Adopt a down-to-earth view of a problem's components, identify and own your and others' role in them, and determine realistically what basic steps are required for survival. This process can be practiced as an exercise—as with resilience engineering—or deployed when facing a real problem in real time.
- **Seek meaning from adversity.** Rather than ask, "Why is this happening?" ask, "What will I learn by suffering through this?" You may find the meaning of true friendship and discover strengths you never knew you had as you wade through adversity. The experience will inform the way you solve problems in the future.

- **Keep your values close.** Staying mindful of your ideals infuses your environment with purpose and meaning, enabling you to shape and interpret events. Keeping focused on an organization's values is even more important for organizational resilience than resilient employees are. Knowing what you (or your organization) will do—and what you (or it) won't do—to solve a problem will inform the best route out of it.
- **Be resourceful.** *Pluck* is when you make do with what you have on hand, and being resilient in this regard (rather than bemoaning your deficits) is important. Being nimble and able to improvise keeps you on the up-and-up, focused on solutions, and moving forward. *Grit* is another attribute of those who persevere despite setbacks. Popularized by MacArthur "genius" Angela Duckworth's *New York Times* bestseller of that title, grit is a special blend of passion and persistence that is an important trait of resilient leaders.
- **Rewrite "negative scripts."** As a friend might say, "If you don't like the play you're in, change the set." How you take responsibility in responding to change puts the onus of control squarely on your shoulders. Don't wait for others to change or merely hope that events will unfold in your favor. Be thoughtful and active in making things better.
- **Accept yourself—and others.** Come to terms with your tendencies, strengths, and vulnerabilities, and forgive yourself and others for their foibles. Lead an authentic life that is consistent with your values. Stand tall in who you are, and be the best version of that person you can.
- **Manage your anger.** Rather than lose control and unleash anger in the moment, call a halt to the situation, take a walk around the block, or seek the listening ear of a trusted confidant. Return to the situation when you are able to address facts assertively but without blaming, to

calmly describe your feelings, and to define what you hope will happen next.

- **Own your mistakes, and then move on.** Rather than blame everything else when things go awry, admit your mistakes and your role in them, and then figure out how to proceed. An error is not confirmation that you are a failure, and it doesn't mean you're unfit for decision making. Sit up straight, apologize (if necessary), and then move on.
- **Be resilient in your life.** Your mother was right. Get enough sleep, eat right, exercise, and be kind to yourself, particularly as you cope with potential stressors.

Tapping inner resilience may feel more awkward to some than to others, but *every* person and *every* organization can learn it—with practice and with the determination and understanding at the outset that change is required.

EXERCISE 1

Write a few paragraphs about a "negative script" in your life. How might you define a new role for yourself? What steps should you take to implement that role? What obstacles might interfere? What is your backup plan?

EXERCISE 2

List three situations where you made a mistake or failed to achieve a goal. Recall how you explained these failures to others and to yourself. What was the worst thing that happened after you made the mistake? In the future, how might you reframe your mistakes and failures?

RESOURCES

Coutu, D. L. 2002. "How Resilience Works." *Harvard Business Review* 80 (5): 46–55.

Duckworth, A. 2016. *Grit: The Power of Passion and Perseverance.* New York: Scribner.

Fontaine, D. K., S. Bauer-Wu, and D. Germano. 2014. "The Architecture of Resilience." Published January 8. www.huffingtonpost.com /dorrie-k-fontaine/the-architecture-of-resil_b_4560762.html.

Hollnagel, E., J. Braithwaite, and R. L. Wears. 2013. *Resilient Health Care.* Burlington, VT: Ashgate Publishing Company.

McBride, A. B. 2011. *The Growth and Development of Nurse Leaders.* New York: Springer.

Manage Your Job

I (KEN) HAVE had *two* best jobs. At the very beginning of my career, starting when I was 18 and for the next five years, I worked as an emergency room orthopedic technician in a hospital in Tulsa, Oklahoma. Responding quickly as part of a team that worked incredibly well together to allay our patients' fears and make them comfortable satisfied my itch to give the very best of myself to our patients. My team members and I (still in touch to this day) not only were proud of our roles, but we also felt we were part of something bigger than ourselves. To an 18-year-old college kid aching to find his way, the job offered an incredible vantage and beginning.

My current position at the University of Virginia (UVA) School of Nursing—I'm associate dean for strategic partnerships and innovation and hold the UVA Medical Center endowed chair in nursing—has been similarly gratifying because I get to spend my days doing what I love most and do best. This job offers autonomy and independence as well as teamwork and camaraderie, and my boss is a visionary and champion without being a micromanager. That I am valued as a person first and foremost, rather than as a producer or a product, is affirming—and it brings out, I believe, my and my colleagues' best performance.

Dorrie has had *many* best jobs, both clinical and academic, but perhaps her all-time favorite was working for six years as an associate dean with Dean Kathy Dracup—an amazing nurse scholar, mentor, and leader—at the University of California, San Francisco (UCSF). Before she left UCSF to become dean of the School of Nursing at

UVA, Dorrie had told Kathy that she hoped to become a dean one day, and Kathy offered to be her mentor.

Working with Kathy made the six years fly by. Dorrie learned incredible lessons, including what the best leaders do to ensure success, how they handle breakdowns and turn them into breakthroughs, and, most of all, how they stay optimistic despite budget cuts and other common snafus. In addition to sharing the inside scoop on what it means to run a top-tier, well-respected school of nursing, Kathy would stop in Dorrie's doorway every morning and say, "I am *so* glad you're here!" Kathy established monthly birthday dinners, hosted in her own home, for staff and faculty (and their significant others) who were celebrating a birthday that month. These events brought together staff and faculty from the most varied backgrounds, and because many would not otherwise have had occasion to meet each other, serendipity led to amazing friendships that made the work back in the office seem to go a little smoother. Dorrie has continued the tradition of these birthday dinners for more than seven years now—and with similar results.

Of course, like everyone, Dorrie and I have also both worked in terrible jobs—under lackluster, narcissistic, ineffective, or temperamental bosses; surrounded by bad conditions; and among unmotivated peers. We've both received superficial performance reviews, had bosses and colleagues who didn't listen, experienced ego-driven personalities, and seen some of the messiest offices in existence. We've both stayed too long in positions, hoping for a turnaround or some luck; and at other moments, we've left too soon for what we thought was a better opportunity that ultimately was not.

All of it—the good and the bad—influenced our paths, this book, and especially this section. We learned that managing yourself first and your job second will give your career the boost it needs to really take off.

So now that you've landed the job you were looking for, how will you make it yours?

—Ken White

Own the Job You Have

Consider every experience, position held, and interaction to be an opportunity to learn and grow. Focus on the task, discussion, role, and job at hand with the intent to do them all well. Be intentional and purposeful in your actions, because everything you do has meaning. Know yourself, and seek opportunities based on who you are, not who you want to be. You would be amazed how my roles as secretary, paralegal, and nurse have helped me be of service in a variety of leadership roles in healthcare. Remember that the next step will always come!

—Michelle D. Hereford, MSHA, RN, FACHE,
chief, community hospitals and post-acute care division,
University of Virginia Health System, Charlottesville

MANY PEOPLE SPEND inordinate time and energy jockeying to get a better, more advanced job before mastering the position they're in. But *every* job has something valuable to teach, whether it's one you plan to keep for two years or two decades, and the best way to advance your career is to do a great job in the position you're in. Give it your all, and absorb every lesson it has to impart. Focus on what's right in front of you before sprinting off in another direction that may (or may not) offer more promise.

So how do you dig into the job you have?

- **Take your organization's mission and vision and "microtize" them to your area of responsibility.** You're there to add value. So it's important to understand your role in helping the organization achieve its objectives. Step one is to fully understand your company's current priorities, as well as its overall strategy and direction. If it's focused on quality improvements, consider what you can do to help reduce errors or improve the patient experience. If its aim is to expand programs to better manage population health, mull over how you might help initiate and lead such growth.
- **Endeavor to go beyond what's expected.** After you're clear on your organization's goals and expectations—being sure to ask for clarification if needed—visualize how a successful year in your position might look. Figure out what you will need to move beyond what's expected of you, and leverage opportunities to exceed expectations. For example, if you recruit a new surgeon doing a novel, much-needed procedure, the increased revenue from the surgeon's activities may help you exceed your profit goals. If you can find two or three such levers, you may be able to plow through and exceed your goals. When your boss asks you for something, get it in on time and give more than was requested. Anticipate what the next logical step will be, and get on it.
- **Change something visible early on.** When you take a new job, try to accomplish something visible in your first few weeks as a symbol of change. Rearrange the furniture, paint the reception room, start daily rounds, or initiate a morning coffee-time team huddle. Talk to your supervisor to find out what's important. Based on what you learn, draft a 30- to 90-day action plan to make an impact, and share the plan with colleagues and supervisors. Keep everyone informed of the progress you make in implementing the plan, and be an expert at managing the details.

- **Be detail oriented.** This point can't be overstated. You want to make a great first impression—and honestly, you get one shot—but nothing ruins your chances of making that impression more than sloppily done, ill-conceived, error-ridden work. Make sure that what you produce is professional in appearance and in the format your supervisor wants. Double-check your facts, spelling, and grammar. And complete your work on time. If you need more time, be transparent about it and discuss an extension. Be certain that your work solves problems and doesn't produce additional tasks for someone else or lead to more questions that need answering. When your supervisor requests a report on a subject, she is asking you to define what this subject means to your organization. Be prepared to give thoughtful, well-researched, in-depth answers, not broad ones.
- **Keep your nose clean.** Don't waste time on gossip or office politics. Idle speculation can do harm. Off-the-cuff remarks and jokes are inappropriate, and work isn't the place for them. If others engage in them, don't get sucked in. Keep focused on your job. Surround yourself with others who do the same. And don't use profanity, even if you think it. It's never appropriate in a healthcare setting, and certainly not from an executive.
- **Ferret out strong colleagues.** Early on in a job, it usually becomes clear who your go-to resources are. Figure out who can help you succeed.
- **Plan ahead.** Anticipate what the organization and your supervisor will need. Think ahead and solve problems.

The best managers and leaders focus on the job in front of them. They give their best effort, thoughtfully solve problems, and invest the time and energy it takes to really tackle a job. And when they do that, promotions and opportunities invariably follow.

EXERCISE 1

Review the Nurse Executive Competencies of the American Organization of Nurse Executives or the Healthcare Executive Competencies Assessment Tool of the American College of Healthcare Executives. Then, identify your areas of strength and weakness. Develop an action plan to turn three weaknesses into strengths.

EXERCISE 2

Ask yourself how you're adding value to your job and organization. How will you be remembered after you have left the organization? Write down ways you would like to be remembered, and then work and behave in ways to make it happen.

RESOURCES

American College of Healthcare Executives (ACHE). 2016. *ACHE Healthcare Executive 2017 Competencies Assessment Tool.* Accessed February 9, 2017. www.ache.org/pdf/nonsecure/careers /competencies_booklet.pdf.

American Organization of Nurse Executives. 2015. *Nurse Executive Competencies.* www.aone.org/resources/nec.pdf.

Drucker, P. F. 2004. "What Makes an Effective Executive?" *Harvard Business Review* 82 (6): 58–63, 136.

Dye, C. F., and A. N. Garman. 2015. *Exceptional Leadership: 16 Critical Competencies for Healthcare Executives,* 2nd ed. Chicago: Health Administration Press.

Maximize the First 90 Days

Before you accept a new leadership position, negotiate the expectations for the first 90 days. Invest time in your new position listening to stakeholders and rounding—and include as many frontline nurses as possible on all shifts. Share a co-created vision, evidence-based practices and benchmark targets for professional nursing, and expectations for a healthy work environment.

—Tina Mammone, PhD, RN, NEA-BC, vice president and chief nursing officer, University of California San Francisco Medical Center, San Francisco

IN THE US Navy, when a new captain takes over a ship, the entire crew assembles to see a physical manifestation of the change of command. The new captain boards the ship as the retiring one disembarks, usually after a handshake and wave, in a ceremony that takes place under the gaze of all the sailors. It is abundantly clear who is now in charge.

Although you may not have the luxury of such a definitive induction ceremony in your new job, a proper beginning will ensure a successful tenure. A rocky start can mean a poor fit or be difficult to recover from (though not always). As the old saying goes, you have but one chance to make a good first impression, so it's important to start a new job carefully, thoughtfully, and properly. Here are a few ideas to guide you in those early days:

- **Understand your role.** Before your first day, you should have a good idea of what those who hired you expect of you. What are the parameters of your authority and responsibilities? Whom do you supervise? What's detailed in your official job description, and which responsibilities of yours may not be so clearly delineated? With time, of course, your role will become more sharply defined. But in those early days, if you are not sure what is expected, ask. Be frank about things that seem confusing or vague. As you gather information, goals—both for yourself and for your organization—will likely crystallize.

- **Articulate your expectations to your staff and to the organization at large.** Call a department meeting early on, and ask for introductions and short background summaries from your colleagues. Offer some information about yourself as well before outlining your general concept of management. Listen attentively, be friendly, and, above all, do your best to appear comfortable even if you don't entirely feel it. Early impressions are often lasting impressions, and it's the rare person who is an affable combination of leader and mentor, listener, and strategist. Do your best to be that person.

- **Observe, listen, and ask.** You may be leading some employees who are older than you and who have years of rich professional experience and perspective. These people are often the individuals from whom you can glean the best, most pertinent, and most useful information. They can be potent allies, too, and some may have seen many executives come and go. Get them on your side by being a thoughtful, responsive listener. Ask them about their projects and see if they have ideas for improving things. Often, people are just waiting for someone to ask their opinion, and they'll relish the chance to offer it. Really listen to the responses you get. The most proficient executives learn to observe, listen, and ask questions well before they act.

- **Study the history and culture of your organization.** Savvy executives alter their focus and approach on the basis of current environmental realities. Tap a few colleagues as advisers who can help you during your first few months to fully understand the organization, where it's coming from, and where it's headed.

- **Gather information for at least a couple of months before instituting transformational change.** Try to find out if the organization has any pressing problems that must be immediately addressed. If so, you may not have the luxury of delaying decisions. Otherwise, wait to act while you gather information.

- **Set goals for yourself and the organization as you begin your new position.** Try to determine what actions are necessary to ensure the organization's success. A few critical questions will guide your goals: What are the most important existing and potential revenue sources? Who are your best and most important customers? Don't try to set too many goals at once—at the outset, three to five are probably enough. As you're marking them, be sure to clearly communicate the goals to the organization, your boss, and your colleagues.

- **Show leadership and professionalism in everything you do.** Your employees and colleagues will be watching and evaluating everything you do, say, and write. Be deliberate—but careful and wise, too. Remember your manners, don't interrupt, and be unfailingly polite. Do your best to remember people's names.

- **Communicate! Communicate! Communicate!** Start your tenure by being a clear and honest communicator. People should understand your messages and will appreciate your transparency. And talk the talk: Make sure that when you say yes, you follow through. The same goes for saying no. If you can't do anything about a problem, say so. Your candor will be remembered—and appreciated.

- **Be visible.** All employees like to see their leaders. On the first day or two, and regularly thereafter, visit all areas and shifts for which you are responsible. Visit areas and meet people who work to support your staff, such as clinical support, registration, case management, and other departments. Word that a new leader is traipsing around will quickly spread. And while you're being visible, introduce yourself to everyone you meet. Ask them what they do for the company, what they like about it, and what they dislike. You should continue these rounds—a critical part of what the best leaders do—throughout your tenure.
- **Ask routinely for a status report from *all* of your stakeholders.** Asking only your high-level advisory group how things are going may not reveal the entire picture. Solicit feedback from a variety of people. Ask, "How are we doing? What mistakes are we making? What can we do better?"

Good planning and execution will ensure that you start your new position in good order. And a good start often leads to a good tenure.

EXERCISE 1

Keep a journal of events that happen in the first 90 days of your tenure, and set a goal for personal action during that period. When you have finished the first 90 days, set your sights on goals for the next 90 days.

EXERCISE 2

During the first 90 days, make a list of all the people you would like to meet during "listening rounds." When you meet with each one, jot down key discussion points. Ask each to name three things that work really well and three things that don't work so well. Before ending each meeting, ask if there is anyone else you should meet with or get to know.

RESOURCES

Stein, M., and L. Christiansen. 2010. *Successful Onboarding: Strategies to Unlock Hidden Value Within Your Organization.* New York: McGraw-Hill.

Watkins, M. 2013. *The First 90 Days: Proven Strategies for Getting Up to Speed, Faster and Smarter.* Boston: Harvard Business Review Press.

Embrace Diversity as Excellence

The need for a diverse nursing workforce has never been greater. Not only do patients want caregivers who look like them and speak their language, but we also cannot reduce health inequities or improve care and patients' health outcomes without a broader view of the world that encompasses differences, understanding, and humility. The goal is to cultivate an environment that openly and honestly respects and engages differences, allowing room for a rich variety of perspectives, beliefs, and experiences. Ideals of inclusion and engagement make for more capable, compassionate, culturally humble, and simply better nurses. This will surely ripple outward to patients, who will be the satisfied recipients of excellent and competent care.

—Susan Kools, PhD, RN, FAAN,
Madge M. Jones Professor of Nursing, associate dean for diversity and inclusion and director of global initiatives, University of Virginia School of Nursing, Charlottesville

AMERICA IS INCREASINGLY a melting pot of richly varied cultures and people with diverse backgrounds, ethnicities, and points of view. As nursing leaders, our purpose is to improve health and to provide quality, equitable care to diverse communities while recognizing, as we hire and promote, that the makeup of our employees should reflect those they serve. Naturally, patients and their families feel most comfortable when those caring for them speak the same language and share a similar heritage or even common physical features. Medical centers and clinics would be prudent to make a concerted effort to connect with a wide variety of patients through thoughtful planning, recruitment, and hiring practices. At the same time, it is crucial for *all* healthcare providers to have deep respect and sensitivity for patients and their families across differences, because complete concordance is not possible.

Historically, *diversity* referred to physical traits that were visible—gender, ethnicity, race, and age, for example. Today, we need a broader perspective on diversity, one that values differences that encompass more than traditional demographics. Many other social characteristics and identities define us as people—including sexual orientation, gender identity, physical ability, socioeconomic status, spirituality, and language—and these intersect and intertwine to shape our life experiences, ideas, and perspectives. When diversity is embraced, it becomes a component of excellence; engagement with diverse people and ideas makes us all better, including our organizations. Promoting a culture of inclusivity, respect, and true engagement across differences in people and ideas allows excellence to happen.

Notable among those calling for change in the way diversity is considered is University of Virginia business professor Martin Davidson, who argues that by considering people's diversity of perspective, experience, and strategy—rather than just their skin color or religion—an organization can widen and strengthen its talent pool. Dr. Davidson joins a growing chorus of individuals hoping to tap differences that aren't so obvious—generational and religious differences as well as those relating to physical ability, sexual orientation, and geographic origin, among others. It's time, asserts Dr. Davidson, for a sea change in the way we leverage diversity: Rather than merely aiming to increase our numbers of women and racial minorities, we must consider diversity as a way to gain a breadth of perspectives different from our own and to break from tradition.

Perhaps John Fitzgerald Gates, associate dean for diversity and engagement at the School of Engineering and Applied Sciences of the University of Virginia, said it best:

> So what must we do to fulfill the promise of diversity? First, we must think bigger when it comes to diversity. Diversity is not about difference; it is about excellence. Everyone and everything can strive to be excellent. Every aspect of our businesses, schools, churches, organizations, and society can be part of an excellence motif. The issue is unlearning our old mental models in which we see diversity as belittling "otherness," and start seeing it instead as representing the best of everything: organizational learning and innovation, business strategy, resource allocation and alignment, structural integration, product development, and leadership integrity.

If you surround yourself with people exactly like you, harmony might ensue—boredom, too—but your growth and potential for innovation will stagnate. In contrast, if you pepper your team with people who bring different ways of thinking—based on their socioeconomic backgrounds, their political or religious views, or their sexual orientation, for example—you'll look through a wider, sharper, more nuanced lens. The work might take more time, but the outcome of a diverse team is often true innovation born of the ability to develop strategies from differences. The best, most effective teams are not filled with yes-men; they're made up of those open to others' wisdom and perspective, who have the ability to consider all avenues before collaborating toward a solution. The result is often innovative and different—and highly successful.

Thus, the notion of diversity for diversity's sake is no longer the goal; diversity is simply good business. With a diverse patient base, hospitals can grow their market share by expanding and highlighting their cultural sensitivity and accommodation and by ensuring the diversity of their workforce, including management. Healthcare organizations can reframe diversity and market it as valuable and part of what makes the organizations excellent.

Only when we recognize and appreciate the value and breadth of our differences can we create better, more thoughtful healthcare systems and services for all our patients. And only when we develop and sustain an organizational culture that identifies strength in differences and promotes inclusion in the workforce can employees be fully engaged. So where do you begin?

Start with yourself. How well do you know yourself? Do you wholly understand how your many life experiences have shaped your perspectives? Are you aware of your values, assumptions, and implicit biases about others and how these affect the people you relate to? Are you inclusive and respectful in your language? Are you mindful of and sensitive to others around you?

After this self-reflection, consider the following areas of diversity, which may help you be more mindful of ways to appreciate differences in and among people:

- **Generational:** Although members of each generation tend to share certain values and attitudes, never assume that certain characteristics "go" with a particular age group. For example, don't assume that your older employee isn't technologically savvy or that your millennial colleague is addicted to social media. Be cognizant of how different generations perceive change, technology, communication, and work–life integration—but acknowledge the individual, not the tenets of the generation to which he belongs (see lesson 28 for more on generational differences).
- **Gender:** Men and women face different challenges in the workplace, and they often work differently and distinctly from one another. Many women (and some men) work full-time while raising a family. If you've got a talented employee, let that person—regardless of gender—go on

and off the fast track to leadership development while raising children, especially in the early years. Talent is rare and worth keeping, and by offering flexibility to working parents early on, you will not only earn their loyalty over time but also find that these individuals are often wizards at time management. Once their children are older and self-sufficient, these moms and dads will likely be among your best assets, and they'll also bring an important perspective as parents.

- **Caregivers:** Similar to caregivers of young children but dramatically less heralded, some workers have the responsibility of caring for their aging or infirm parents. These individuals have both special needs and perspectives that can be hugely important for a healthcare setting. Tap them for their wisdom, and regularly ask how they're doing and how their parent is faring. Building loyalty will boost caregivers' confidence that their perspective is critical—that they're valued not only for their work but also for their special vantage on the aging process and its inherent challenges.
- **Minorities and other cultures:** Offer extra support to new minority hires and to employees from different cultures, and be interested and inquisitive (without being obtrusive) about their perspectives, traditions, and backstories. Implement initiatives that support talented minority employees—such as formal mentorship programs and flexibility to attend religious or ethnic functions that may not be on everyone's calendar—to be sure you retain them.
- **Disabilities:** One of the nation's largest minority groups consists of people with disabilities. The Americans with Disabilities Act requires employers to provide certain accommodations to employees living with disabilities. But providing special physical and emotional support, both to employees with disabilities and to those caring for family members with disabilities, further enhances organizational

sensitivity. Such support might be something as simple as walking alongside a slower-moving colleague with multiple sclerosis during a fire drill, allowing the parent of a child with cerebral palsy to telecommute, or holding the door for a peer who uses a cane. If you just think about the ways, large and small, that you can make life easier for those dealing with disabilities, you'll cultivate warmth and loyalty—and your organization will be the better for it.

- **LGBT (lesbian, gay, bisexual, and transgender):** Whether LGBT professionals self-identify or not, they're often overlooked in traditional diversity programs. To promote an inclusive and accepting work environment, sponsoring Safe Space training programs may be useful. Be an example of acceptance and warmth when you meet same-sex partners and spouses—others will take their cue from your behavior and follow suit. Be aware of the special accommodations needed for transgender employees who are in the midst of transition; model respect, and expect it of others in the organization.

- **Veterans:** Most veterans have great skills, but some experience great difficulty in getting a chance to apply them in the workplace. Roughly 1 percent of the American population has served in the armed forces, and many individuals and organizations already make a concerted effort to support veterans in other ways. Offering them work may be one of the best ways to salute them.

As you aim to support those working in your organization and welcome the richness of diversity that each brings, remember that *what* you say and *how* you say it are often just as important as your actions. Use inclusive language, be sensitive to and respectful of differences, and be careful not to offend. If you don't know the best way to demonstrate inclusion through language, ask. If you make a mistake, acknowledge it and apologize.

Using nonspecific words such as *partner* or *spouse* is the best way to invite couples to the summer barbeque or staff retreat luncheon. Avoid slang and derogatory words entirely. Being openly supportive of your rich variety of colleagues will prompt others around you to do the same.

Finally, know your people. Even if your organization is a big one, make an effort to know a little about everyone on a personal level. Be accepting of who they are, where they come from, and what they bring. Doing so will push your organization's ethos in the direction of acceptance and transform it into a place that is successfully leveraging the differences within.

EXERCISE 1

Assess the characteristics of your staff. Think beyond visible demographics such as age, gender, race, and ethnicity to the other diverse characteristics and perspectives they bring to your organization. Now assess your patient base. What are the gaps in diversity that you have to address to ensure the care needs of your patients are met?

EXERCISE 2

Explore your implicit bias by taking one of Project Implicit's implicit associations tests. Encourage your colleagues to do so, too. Even better, organize a class in which you and your colleagues take the test individually but discuss implicit biases as a group.

RESOURCES

Davidson, M. N. 2011. *The End of Diversity as We Know It: Why Diversity Efforts Fail and How Leveraging Difference Can Succeed.* San Francisco: Berrett-Koehler Publishers.

Gates, J. F. 2014. "Do We Really Need 'Diversity' Offices?" Updated September 6. www.huffingtonpost.com/john-fitzgerald-gates -phd/do-we-really-need-diversi_b_5564723.html.

Kools, S., and D. K. Fontaine. 2016. "Nursing Diversity: Why Back- stories Matter." Updated January 25. www.huffingtonpost.com /susan-kools-rn-phd-faan/nursing-diversity_b_8890942.html.

Project Implicit. 2011. "Take a Test." Accessed July 31, 2016. https://implicit.harvard.edu/implicit/takeatest.html.

Organize Your Workspace

In my first job, I was immediately assigned charge nurse duties on a busy telemetry unit. Organization and prioritization skills were critical to the effective management of patient care—and they took practice. That experience in developing systems for organization helped transform the way in which I operate as a leader.

Much has been written about the liberating effects of tidiness and living and working clutter free. Reducing clutter helps me focus on the aesthetics that surround me. In my office, I display a few pieces of art that bring me joy and positive energy. Earned diplomas, awards, and recognitions bring me immense pride, but I don't adorn my office walls with them because, as a leader and colleague, I want my office to be about the people I am meeting with, not about me.

—Tracy Kemp Stallings, BSN, RN, MSHA, director of industry engagement, Department of Health Administration, Virginia Commonwealth University, Richmond

YOU MAY BE an exceptional time manager and a beloved boss, and you may set robust priorities, but what's in the top drawer of your desk? How does your desktop (both literal and electronic) appear at the beginning, middle, and end of the day? How organized is your briefcase, handbag, or glove box, and how filthy is your office coffee mug?

Although successful and professionally gifted individuals occupy the entire spectrum of tidiness and organization—from neat-freak immaculates to scattered and downright slobs—how well you keep house in your office says a lot about you. Improving your organizational skills may have a positive impact on your productivity, efficiency, stress level, and overall effectiveness. All it takes is being thoughtful, regimented, and neat!

The first question to ask is how you feel your office space is working for you. Can you find what you need when you need it? Do you have systems in place that help you prioritize, recall important meetings and events, and tally what you've done versus what still needs doing? Do you have files for bigger-picture projects and logs for inspiring articles and ideas that might inform your organization's wider vision and goals? And if you don't, do you mind?

If you're like many of us, your office could use some real thought and tidying up. Here are a few questions to consider at the outset:

- Are your desk, computer monitor, chair, and ancillary furniture (guest chairs, lighting, shelves, and so on) configured appropriately?
- Is your phone situated relative to your handedness (i.e., to the right if you're right-handed)?
- Are your trash can and recycling bin both accessible to you and cloaked from others?
- Is your furniture comfortable and ergonomically designed so that your posture is preserved?
- If it's useful in your role, do you have a place to meet other than your desk and a guest chair (a small table with chairs, perhaps)?

Your office says a lot about you—including its physical appearance, setup, and organization—so try to imagine the picture it conveys, and decide whether that picture matches the one you want people to take away as an impression when they meet with you there.

Your office should also serve as a haven for you to do good work with minimal distractions and maximum comfort. Although your space should set a professional tone and have the requisite comforts you require, you may want to add a few personal touches—not only to boost your sense of well-being but also to offer a bit of yourself to others. Family photos, framed art, your diplomas, or a plant all offer nice touches. So do small collections of items from your professional work, such as books you've authored, awards you've won, or pictures of you with colleagues at conferences. You should enjoy the space and make sure it works for you.

Now consider what you see. Are papers everywhere? Are files you haven't touched in years still lying in view? Could those empty cabinets hold archives that don't need to be a reach away?

If so, consider these tips:

- **Unclutter your desk.** Drawers are for items you don't use every day, so purge what you can and tuck only what's necessary inside a drawer within easy reach. Toss duplicates and anything you no longer need, such as year-old periodicals, outdated books, and files that support old projects. The paper clutter that occupies the top layer of your desk can largely be eliminated given that almost everything today exists in electronic format.

  One organized hospital CEO puts all the papers on her desk away before leaving for the day, a habit she cultivated early on while working for a major in the US Army. The major had the rather nasty habit of sweeping papers left on his subordinates' desks at day's end into their trash cans or onto the floor. Although the habit of an end-of-the-day paperless desk was force-fed by a demanding boss, the CEO maintains today that she's better for it because it forced her to deal with every paper on her desk and to get things done. She says it also ensures that she excavates through layers to be sure nothing has been buried or forgotten, and it enables her to make the next day's to-do list.

- **Unclutter your computer desktop.** By now, most people know that saving documents, e-mail attachments, photos, and articles onto one's computer desktop is both a confusing and a technologically ill-advised way to work—and yet, most of us do it. An overabundance of desktop files clogs your visual field, creates issues with older and newer versions, and slows your machine down. Put electronic documents in file folders in a safe and appropriate place right away. If you do it correctly the first time, you won't need to drag and drop stuff onto your desktop that will only be ignored, become irritating, and slow your machine down.

- **Develop a good filing system.** Every job requires a seamless way to keep paper and electronic documents organized. Don't put this task off; as soon as you begin a job, figure out what you need to save, how you need to save it, where it should exist, and what the names of the folders (electronic and paper) ought to be. Position those used regularly close at hand—on your right, for example, if you're right-handed.

  - Keep file names obvious, and include dates if appropriate. If you give file folders vague and undescriptive names, such as "Jeff's file" or "2014 projects," you will forget what the files contain and never be able to retrieve the right information. Consider using major categories and subcategories—for example, "Surgery–Operating Budget," "Surgery–Capital Equipment," and "Surgery–Nurse Recruitment."

  - Organize electronic files that need regular archiving by month and year. Having a "Done" file alongside your "Pending" file is sometimes prudent, especially for regular tasks.

  - If you have an administrative assistant, consider using paper folders with each day's items organized according to the day of the week.

- If you have direct reports and meet with them regularly, create a paper file for each individual, and drop in notes as they occur to you so that you can bring them up for discussion at your next meeting.
- To deal with some of the barrage of mail and paperwork that comes your way, create a reading file that contains nonurgent information that you can review while waiting for a flight, taking a taxi, or sitting on the train.
- If you need to retain files for a designated period, mark them with destruction dates. Most healthcare organizations have policies on retention of records, but destruction dates are easily and often overlooked.
- Keep a paper file on your own accomplishments, dropping in information as you go on what you've done, what impact it's had, how you've been recognized, and so on. Many companies require employees at all levels to complete a self-assessment and detail their accomplishments prior to their annual review, and keeping a personal file is a great way to have perfect recall when you complete this task or update your resume.
- Maintain the filing system you develop. After all, a system is only as good as its owner.
- **Keep priorities and to-do lists visible.** Update them often. Whether on paper or in an electronic document, keep your top three to five priorities for the day close to your visual field. "Out of sight, out of mind" applies here: Visual reminders—and they can be simple—keep you on task, and it's always satisfying to check off what you've accomplished before moving on to what's next.
- **Know who's doing what.** For bigger projects, keep a record of what you have delegated to whom, and when it's due. Ticklers—such as a note on your calendar to follow up on something or a jotted-down due date with a "soft"

deadline a week or so in advance of the "hard" deadline—
are useful for keeping track of this information.

- **Use a system to keep track of ideas you have while on
  the go.** If you have a mobile device, use it to take notes
  if you're somewhere where a pen, paper, or computer is
  not available. Keep a pen and paper near your bed and in
  your car, and use them whenever ideas occur to you for
  projects. Schedule a regular time to retrieve these ideas
  and notes—the beginning and end of the day tend to be
  good—to keep a tally of your thoughts and the tasks that
  need to be accomplished.

- **Keep private things private.** Others who meet with you
  in your office may be able to see documents and messages
  on your computer monitor that they really shouldn't be
  privy to. Therefore, consider using a screen to protect the
  privacy of your documents. Alternatively, you could also
  simply ensure your computer screen is always turned away
  from the direct view of your guests.

- **Conquer your calendar.** Rather than keep separate
  calendars at work and home, integrate the two. If you use
  the calendar on your mobile device, it will always be close
  at hand. Add standing meetings, birthdays, anniversaries,
  annual conferences, and other important dates as recurring
  events so that they populate automatically.

- **Stay charged.** You need three cords to keep your mobile
  device charged. Have two cords for regular electrical
  outlets—one at home and one in the office. The third cord
  is a special charging apparatus for use in your car. Keep
  each cord where it belongs. Two at home and one in the
  car won't do you a lick of good if you're in your office.

- **Follow daily rituals.** Schedule time each day for reading
  and returning e-mails, returning phone calls, and making
  rounds, and limit yourself to the times scheduled. Build in
  extra time for traveling to meetings and to ensure you're
  not late to work because traffic is bad or you need to stop

for gas. Schedule at least one hour a day to take care of work at your desk so that you can reorient yourself to your priorities and prepare for upcoming deadlines and meetings.

- **End each day by prepping for the following one.** End-of-day rituals should include clearing your desk, putting items back in their places, and reviewing your calendar for the next day.

The effort you put into creating and maintaining an efficient workspace will pay off hugely if you simply make sure to follow the structure you have set up. Instead of spending time and energy looking for things and moving piles from one spot to the next, you'll be able to focus on productivity—and enjoy the space you've created.

EXERCISE 1

Examine your system for organizing electronic files on your computer. What are you doing well? What could you do better?

EXERCISE 2

Schedule a time to declutter your office. Recycle books, shred documents, and either file papers or discard them. Plan to do this at least annually.

RESOURCE

Online Business Buddy. 2013. *Organize Your Office: The Ultimate Guide to Organizing Your Office and Having a Stress-Free Workplace*, Kindle edition. Amazon Digital Services, Inc.

Identify and Support Culture

In my nursing leadership career, two axioms have assisted me in supporting, understanding, or changing an organization's culture: "With great power comes great responsibility" and "Culture eats strategy." Before changing or empowering a culture, leaders must take time to understand that culture. They must listen, review, and assess how their employees interact with and respond to each other and their patients. Observing, listening, and understanding an organization's culture take time, but it is time well spent. Once the culture is understood, a wise approach to implementing projects, goals, and strategy is to leverage strengths in the culture. When this process is overlooked or skipped, culture will eat strategy. Many leadership books advise against making any changes in the first 90 days of a new job or assignment. I have found it takes at least that long to truly get a handle on an organization's culture, norms, and beliefs.

—Genemarie McGee, MS, RN, NEA-BC,
chief nursing officer, Sentara Healthcare, Norfolk, Virginia

THINK ABOUT THE best job you've ever had. Then consider the reasons it was the best. Ten to one, it had something to do with the feel of the place—that difficult-to-pin-down warmth and collegiality of peers, the drive and vision of your supervisor and fellow nurses, the fun you had tackling work challenges independently and in groups, or perhaps the satisfaction of finding solutions to the problems at hand. That *je ne sais quoi* is workplace culture.

But what goes into a hospital's or company's culture—its feel—isn't so easy to pin down. Managers have something to do with it, as do a company's mission, vision, and goals. Employees play a large part, too.

One of the most rewarding routes to success is to have a hand in nurturing a great workplace culture. In healthcare, given the nobility of purpose—health, wellness, and caring, for starters—you've got a natural leg up on developing a positive culture because, at base, the field centers on helping people. But as a nurse leader, you're responsible for filling in the rest and making your organization one that people will love, work hard in, and feel great loyalty to.

Do whatever you can to cultivate a place where employees are happy, loyal, and engaged and where they feel empowered to make positive contributions. As you advance in your career and take on greater leadership roles and responsibilities, you will increasingly have opportunities to guide your organization's culture—but early on, you can make a real mark by making your organization a place people feel welcome in and loyal to and where they *want* to come to work.

We all know organizations whose employees are happy and work hard to make the hospital, academic setting, or company successful. These companies have a great workplace culture. So how did they get there?

- **Strong leadership.** A leader sets expectations and creates an environment in which staffers carry out the company's values in clear, coherent, and visible fashion by fulfilling clearly articulated goals. But not even the best leaders can constantly monitor their staff's behaviors and practices day in and day out. When peers hold one another accountable to organizational values and standards, a workplace culture is strong. And when people see their colleagues treating patients with care and respect, picking up the phone on the first ring, holding doors open, and greeting colleagues cheerfully in the corridor, they feel the tide of positivity and pride in their organization. There is buy-in. But how do you get there?

- **Agency and ownership.** Staff must have a say in the values and standards that a company puts in place. Frontline staff who interact directly with patients will embrace values and standards if they helped shape and define those measures as part of a formalized, thoughtful process. Employees don't want to feel they're simply doing a job, clocking in and then clocking out. They want to feel they're stakeholders in a positive, well-vetted vision and to enjoy long, meaningful careers with the company.

- **A bottom-up approach.** Although a strong leader drives an organization's mission, vision, and goals, a company's culture really takes hold when it has buy-in from the population of workers. Therefore, culture cannot be driven from the top down. To be a useful and powerful management tool, culture must be implemented through employee belief and participation.

At every stage of your career, you'll want to spend your days in a hospital or organization that has a healthy work environment—one where respect, trust, and values such as excellence are celebrated (see lesson 45). If you find yourself in one that does not measure up, then you have two choices: (1) make your best contribution by assessing what's going on, aligning with others across disciplines up and down the organization, and developing a plan to make the place better, or (2) leave the unhealthy environment. A wise leader will first attempt to work through a challenging situation. Your first position in nursing should be thoughtfully chosen. Finding a nurse manager who truly cares about growing and nurturing staff is one way to ensure a strong first job.

If choosing your early jobs carefully is so important, how do you discern the corporate culture of an organization you're considering joining? A lot is evident just by looking around. As you tread through the parking lot and enter the building, what do you see? Do employees scurry around with their eyes cast down, or do they look up and smile? Do you see people wasting time, huddled together in corners, or do they appear purposeful and busy? Are there boatloads of new or temporary workers, or do you meet veteran employees with tenure and perspective? Those are all clues.

Another way to assess a hospital's or company's culture is to review its mission statement and compare it with what you see. Who are the company's owners and leaders? When you meet with them, do they know and embody their own mission statement? Is the mission statement succinct and easy to remember?

Before you take a job at any organization, try to imagine how you'll fit in and whether you're a good match for the place. Are the job descriptions clear and well organized, or are the expectations nebulous and vague? Do you fully understand the job's parameters after you've asked? Will there be an orientation or a residency program? Are mentors available who can ease you into your role?

Keep the following tactics in mind:

- **Cultivate and leverage your professional network.** Seek out people who work in organizations that interest you to gain their perspective. If you don't already know someone there, an acquaintance likely has a connection, and online tools such as LinkedIn offer another route to identifying and networking with people in hospitals or companies that interest you.
- **Gain the perspective of the general public.** Ask people how an organization that interests you is regarded in the community. Alternatively, seek out Magnet-designated hospitals, which are known to have met certain rigorous requirements for staffing and patient outcomes, among other criteria, and are therefore "magnets" for nurses.
- **Conduct online research and media searches.** Online local news outlets and media coverage can provide excellent insight into an organization's culture and

priorities and the public's opinion of it. How does it handle negative publicity? How accessible and well spoken are its leaders? What problems has it faced, and what successes has it enjoyed?

EXERCISE 1

Write a paragraph describing your organization's culture. Identify its mission, vision, and goals. How does the culture of the organization affect the employees' work?

EXERCISE 2

Create a personal mission statement and detail what your values are. To gauge your compatibility, compare and contrast your personal mission and values with those of organizations that interest you.

EXERCISE 3

Ask to meet with nurse leaders who have been successful and whom you admire. Ask them what's special about their organization, how they make it special, and what they consider to be the top five ingredients in creating a positive culture. Study their approach by mapping out the route they took in establishing a strong workplace culture.

RESOURCES

McKinnon, T. 2013. "How to Build a Great Company Culture." *Forbes.* Posted October 4. www.forbes.com/sites/group think/2013/10/04/how-to-build-a-great-company-culture/.

Oehlert, J. K. 2015. "Themes in Health Care Culture: Application of Cultural Transformation Theory." *Interdisciplinary Journal of Partnership Studies* 2 (1), article 6.

Patrick, J. 2013. "The Real Meaning of Corporate Culture." *The New York Times* Blog. Posted May 21. http://boss.blogs.nytimes .com/2013/05/21/the-real-meaning-of-corporate-culture.

Shirey, M. R. 2009. "Authentic Leadership, Organizational Culture, and Healthy Work Environments." *Critical Care Nursing Quarterly* 32 (3): 189–98.

Improve Quality and Safety

Nurses are patients' best hope—but we have yet to realize our full potential. Our knowledge, skills, and proximity to patients put us in the best position to ensure all patients receive high-quality, safe, and evidence-based care. The nursing process provides a useful framework for identifying and rectifying problems with care. The public has long trusted the nursing profession above all others; in their most vulnerable state, patients and families count on us to advocate on their behalf. Yet, research studies show we have unfinished business. As nurses, we have the opportunity and the obligation to learn and apply the latest techniques to optimize care and the patient experience.

—Christopher R. Friese, PhD, RN, AOCN, FAAN, professor, University of Michigan School of Nursing, Ann Arbor

YOUR MOST IMPORTANT job as a nurse leader is to ensure the safety of patients, employees, and visitors—essentially everyone who enters your organization's work environment. Immediate correction of threats to quality and safety comes before any other priority. Work on the organization's goals, vision, and long-term strategy cannot proceed until everyone is safe.

Today's nurse leaders must have a solid perspective on care delivery processes and evidence-based clinical guidelines to fully understand the route to the best, safest, and highest-quality care. They must comprehend how to improve, step by step, the quality of care given to all patients and how to ensure that safety remains paramount in an organization's ethos. Because you will likely be held increasingly responsible not only for your hospital's financial outcomes but for its clinical ones as well, taking an active role in understanding processes and procedures is a solid first step toward asserting your commitment to the place and its people.

Consider the following points as you prepare for increasing responsibility as a leader:

- **Know what it means.** Knowing nursing vocabulary isn't enough. To become an expert, you also need to study quality and safety as a subject matter topic, reading case studies that describe which initiatives have worked well for organizations of various types and sizes, which attempts at improvement have failed, and why. Take time to understand the relevant terminology as you do your research. You should be able to read and understand the quality and safety indicators that are driven by the Centers for Medicare & Medicaid Services and various third-party contracts and agreements. If you are working in a hospital or other provider institution, there is likely a series of documents that explicitly state how quality and safety are practiced and measured. Find them and pore over them. The more you read, the more you'll know. Absorb everything you can in this area.

- **Develop a culture of improvement.** As you work to make things better, involve everyone—from the board of trustees on down. Tell them what you think needs work in the areas of quality and safety, and listen intently to what they believe are areas of strength and deficit in this regard. Be open and honest about your organization's shortcomings, and join your colleagues in seeking solutions. Ingrain the importance of specific, visible programs—for example, nurses might wear a fluorescent sash as a sign of concentration as they measure outpatient medications so that others don't interrupt them. As new ideas take root, talk candidly about how a particular initiative is going. Express your continued reliance on your colleagues, and remind them repeatedly that an open, communicative culture is the best first step toward making thoughtful, prudent, lasting change.

- **Express quality and safety in financial terms.** In addition to being the right thing to do, doing something right the first time is always most cost-effective. Preventable errors can lead to everything from a poor organizational reputation for quality to fines, bad press, and lawsuits. Let your colleagues and employees understand the financial fallout from errors in a dollars-and-cents manner by giving them examples. For example, *Each of the _____ hospital-acquired infections at one local medical center cost it more than $_____ million. Unnecessary duplication of medical procedures cost the patient $_____ as well as untold wasted hours and stress.* Institutions follow their quality indicators closely because payments from federal, state, and various third-party sources are increasingly based on quality and safety. Quality and safety matter for myriad reasons—including the bottom line. Express it as such.

- **Look for sustainable, systematic solutions to problems.** Stop the immediate threat, of course, before changing the system so that the threat does not recur. Take care not to overcomplicate it—often, the best solutions are simple, inexpensive, and easy to implement. Got a hand-washing compliance problem? Place signage outside and inside the room, along with sinks and soap. Encourage patients to ask nurses and physicians whether they've washed their hands. Institute other best practices for hand hygiene, and monitor compliance at random times.

- **Continually improve.** If patient falls appear to be on the rise on a particular unit, dig into the situation, determine the cause of the increase, and then improve the process to prevent future falls. Don't overlook simple solutions, though they may not always solve the entire problem. The solution may be as simple as changing the brand of floor wax or the floor-cleaning schedule. Or perhaps an increasing number of elderly patients are being treated in a particular wing of the hospital, or nursing staff have too high a patient load. Training in Lean and Six Sigma improvement methodologies may help solve safety and quality problems such as these.
- **Plan, practice, and measure.** A good plan is a key component of a successful safety program. Make yours as thoughtful and responsive to all facets of the problem as possible. As you develop your plan, make sure it's current with best practices and continually followed up and improved on. Pay close attention to details as you examine an issue before determining a course of action. After you create a plan, monitor the issue and watch for improvements.

  Thus, if your hospital has a growing problem with infections, it may stem from something as basic as poor hand washing or lackluster care of medical instruments. At the outset, you might ask what procedures and reminders are in place for hand-washing compliance and stethoscope cleaning. Then you might inquire about institutional benchmarks and look at the ways other organizations have solved similar issues to prevent infection. What are the hand-washing benchmarks? What changes can your organization make to improve your results? How will you measure whether you're moving the needle in a positive direction?
- **Report your results.** What gets measured gets improved. Insist on transparency, even if the issue is a sensitive one. (*All* issues are likely sensitive, so you'd best be open about

everything.) Share the shortcomings with your colleagues and employees, and impress on them the success that you hope procedural improvements will bring.

- **Develop the personal skills needed to improve safety and quality.** Ensure that both you and the members of your team have the knowledge and skills needed to undertake improvements.
    - Familiarize yourself with the initiatives of the Institute for Healthcare Improvement (IHI).
    - Learn about Lean or Six Sigma improvement techniques.
    - Enhance your financial understanding of value-based purchasing and its connection to quality outcomes and patient satisfaction.
    - Support and work with interprofessional teams to identify opportunities for improvement.
    - Support regular training programs for all staff. Quality and safety depend on the best available evidence and successful practices. Continuing education programs— such as workshops, lectures, retreats, and professional development days—are essential for everyone.
- **Link quality and safety to evidence-based practice.** Not only must care be safe and of high quality, but it also must be the *right* care, proven through scientific evidence to produce the best outcomes.

Above all, develop a passion for improving quality and promoting safety throughout your career as a nurse leader. It is, after all, the most basic, fundamental way to help.

EXERCISE 1

Identify a process in your organization that needs improving, taking notes on what you observe. Is the intensive care unit rife with dissonant, impossible-to-locate patient alarms that fatigue the ears of staff and patients? Are patients not sleeping in the labor and delivery unit because of doors slamming and elevators chirping? Is the emergency room waiting area backlogged for hours with sick people? Are reception staff overwhelmed and terse? Jot down a list of red flags and try to identify some possible solutions.

EXERCISE 2

Earn an IHI Open School Basic Certificate in Quality and Safety.

RESOURCES

Institute for Healthcare Improvement (IHI). 2016. "Open School." Accessed July 18. www.ihi.org/education/ihiopenschool/Pages /default.aspx.

White, K. R., and J. R. Griffith. 2016. *The Well-Managed Healthcare Organization*, 8th ed. Chicago: Health Administration Press.

Listen to Your Stakeholders

"Just ask." Two simple words, yet they imply so much more. The respect and concern you convey by active listening is exponential. Targeted, open-ended questions help, but mostly an unhurried, quietly attentive, honest, and engaged listening approach makes all the difference. Make it a habit!

—Nancy Howell Agee, MSN, RN,
president and CEO, Carilion Clinic, Roanoke, Virginia,
and chair (2018), American Hospital Association

IF HEALTHCARE ORGANIZATIONS aim to serve their communities with the best, highest-quality care, a manager's very first priority must be to determine what's working and what's not. Those we serve—our patients, customers, stakeholders, clients, or whatever you choose to call them—hold the key to helping us understand where and how to improve and, ultimately, how to be more successful. Based on the answers they provide, it's up to the healthcare organization's managers to identify improvements so that the quality of connections within is exceptional, compassionate, and informed by the very best practices.

So what's the best way to find out what customers want? It's simple: Just ask. But figuring out whom to ask, and how, is less straightforward. Unlike a traditional business, which sells products or services to a particular constituent, healthcare delivery is complex, as is a healthcare organization's customer base. For-profit businesses fill their coffers by keeping customers happy to ensure they continue spending. Healthcare organizations, however, have a far nobler purpose: to make people and their communities healthier. And although the patient is a customer, so are a host of others.

Healthcare employees are stakeholders because they're the ones who provide the services as agents of the owners. Physicians are stakeholders because they choose where to refer their patients for healthcare. Insurance companies are stakeholders because they shop around for the best, most profitable provider contracts. Employers are stakeholders because they pay for the bulk of the costs related to their employees' health insurance. Thus, a host of stakeholders and decision makers must be considered in the mix—well before a customer ever presents himself as a patient.

Getting close to your customers in healthcare, then, means listening to everyone. So how, exactly, do you do that? Break it down. Begin with the three most important groups, as described below. As you connect with people both within and outside your organization, consider these five steps to guide your interaction: Ask. Listen. Think. Care. Respond.

- **Patients and their families.** Talk to patients on your rounds. Introduce yourself, and ask open-ended questions such as "How are we doing?" Listen intently to what they say, taking notes and showing you care. If they offer specific complaints (e.g., rotten parking, slow nurse responsiveness, complicated billing issues, difficult wayfinding), follow up with them to tell them how you solved their problems and concerns, if you have done so. If you can't solve their problems, let them know you've listened and are considering ways to make the services better. Leave them with a business card, genuine gratitude, and the sense that they've offered you something extremely important—which they have.

Cultivate a particular vein of conversation with patients and families if you're looking for feedback on specific initiatives. You might ask questions such as the following:

— "We are proud of the compassionate care we offer here, and I wondered what you thought of it?"
— "If there was one thing that might have made your experience here more positive, what would it be? How would it benefit you?"
— "Have we made you feel safe and well cared for here? What specifics made the difference?"
— "Were there particular staff who impressed you (and may I pass on the compliment)?"

- **Employees and volunteers.** Leaders and managers exist to solve problems so that employees on the front lines of a healthcare organization can do what they do best: offer the most compassionate and highest-quality patient-centered care they're capable of. These individuals play a critical role as they deliver small and large kindnesses that are remembered in ways that the actions of surgeons, specialists, and administrators often aren't recalled. Frontline staff are truly every healthcare organization's lifeblood, its foundation, and the key to extraordinary quality and service.

    A successful patient-centered organization is also an employee-focused organization. Connect with your employees, take time to get to know them, and respond to them. Employees who feel valued, listened to, well supported, and personally cared for will not only be immensely loyal to your organization but will also pay these kindnesses forward to their patients and their patients' families. A good way to start a dialogue with employees and volunteers on your rounds is to ask, "Do you have the tools you need to do your job?" Additional questions might include the following:

- "What bogs you down or gets in your way of doing your best?"
- "What are some of the concerns you hear from your patients about the hospital? What concerns do you perceive your colleagues have? What are your concerns?"
- "How can managers like me be of better service to you? What can we do to offer you a platform for even better performance?"
- "What's your favorite part of your job? Who are your favorite colleagues?"
- "What skills could you learn that would help you feel more competent and confident in your job?"
- "Are there other responsibilities or projects here you'd like to be involved in?"

- **Other stakeholders.** Just as important as patients/families and employees/volunteers are the physicians who operate in and around your organization. You must make a Herculean effort to stay close to these physicians (see lesson 30), listen to their needs and concerns, and respond to those concerns competently, effectively, and promptly. Other key stakeholders with whom you should conduct listening rounds include community leaders, referring physicians and provider organizations, and policymakers (including elected government representatives, from your city's mayor to your state and federal representatives and senators). Listen as well to members of the media, your organization's board, donors, suppliers, payers, and anyone else who is connected to or has a stake in your community's health and well-being.

  Get better at listening to this third catch-all group by means of the following:
  - Figure out how to have fewer meetings so that you can conduct rounds more often and thereby identify opportunities for improvement in real time.

- Schedule time to meet with customers. Make sure all the members of your team schedule time to meet with customers, too.
- Include hospitality among your organization's values. Treat those in your organization—whether they work there or are merely stepping across its threshold—as you would if they were special guests in your home. Make sure they feel both safe and welcome.
- Arrange and participate in ongoing professional development for all stakeholders on resilience, collaboration, and sound communication techniques. (Topics to explore might include how to handle difficult conversations, how to be a better team player, or how to practice gentle yoga.) Provide incentives (e.g., food, professional development credit, free parking) to get people in the door, and require a level of participation from staff that is doable and not an encumbrance.
- Learn all you can about active listening—fully concentrating, understanding, and remembering what is said—and then practice, practice, practice.

In healthcare, the only constant is change, so it's critical to consider what's happening from *all* angles. Inexperienced managers commonly listen to one side's story and then start making changes without considering the effect those changes may have on other departments or even on the organization's strategic focus. Don't promise to fix something for someone until you get all the facts and the entire story—otherwise, you'll find yourself spinning your wheels and stirring up ire among groups you hadn't meant to affect.

The whole point of listening, of course, is to help your organization deliver on its mission more effectively. And although you won't be able to solve all the problems you encounter or give everyone every item on their wish lists, if you connect your decisions to your organization's mission, vision, values, and goals, you'll have been true to your role as a transformational leader. Opening lines of communication, gathering information, and then using that information to influence how decisions are made are as critical to an organization's success as its cash flow, operations, marketing, and strategic planning. Your role fuses the bottom line with your organization's heart.

EXERCISE 1

Set aside one hour three times a week to make rounds for the sole purpose of listening to patients, employees, physicians, and other stakeholders. Meet them where they are—on patient units, in the cafeteria, in the surgery lounge, or in their offices. Ask open-ended questions, taking notes as you listen intently to their answers, and identify ways—big or small—to improve operations and to make their jobs and lives easier.

EXERCISE 2

Read a book or take a course on active listening.

RESOURCES

Chapman, S. G. 2012. *The Five Keys to Mindful Communication: Using Deep Listening and Mindful Speech to Strengthen Relationships, Heal Conflicts, and Accomplish Your Goals.* Boston: Shambhala Publications.

Freeman, R. E., J. S. Harrison, and A. C. Wicks. 2007. *Managing for Stakeholders: Survival, Reputation, and Success.* New Haven, CT: Yale University Press.

Hoppe, M. 2011. *Active Listening: Improve Your Ability to Listen and Lead.* Greensboro, NC: Center for Creative Leadership.

Manage Your Messaging

Communication management is a critical skill, and one that improves with practice and reflective feedback from peers and others you trust. Maya Angelou astutely observed that "people will forget what you said, people will forget what you did, but people will never forget how you made them feel." As leaders, we are charged with motivating, inspiring, and supporting staff to make change, grow, improve, and continuously learn. How we communicate, when we communicate, and the way our communication is received make all the difference in what we are trying to accomplish through our messaging. The best way to ensure your message is received the way you intend it is to solicit feedback, reflect on that feedback, and adjust your communication style accordingly.

— Anne Gross, PhD, RN, FAAN, senior vice president
for patient care services and chief nursing officer,
Dana Farber Cancer Institute, Boston, Massachusetts

A GIFTED FORMER student was a top achiever in our graduate management program, and as a nurse manager she had a lot of potential to advance professionally into more senior-level positions. What held her back, she confided, was her inability to communicate well and to think, as she described it, "on her feet."

She wasn't being modest or self-deprecating. Her deficit went well beyond a fear of public speaking: She lacked the confidence, organization, and quality control to offer strong, succinct messages to her audiences. She couldn't articulate quickly, convey her meaning clearly, or express herself in a manner that rallied and inspired her colleagues.

Fast-forward 15 years, however, and she had become a hospital CEO who appeared often in TV news interviews with poise, expressive body language, and an engaging pitch and tone. In addition to these superficial aspects of communication style, she had the ability to send clear, concise, and understandable messages that were appropriately geared to her audience. So what had happened? Plain and simple: She had worked on her messaging skills, simplified and honed her messages, studied best practices—and improved dramatically.

Some people are naturals at sending meaningful, articulate, eloquent, and well-crafted messages, always knowing what to say and how to say it. They understand and use messaging to get power, exert influence, and obtain leverage. The rest of us? We have to practice, as the former student did, to make our messaging stronger.

To succeed as a manager, of course, you have to communicate effectively. When you're in a management or leadership position, others look to you for direction, for inspiration, and for information. And, obviously, it's not only *what* you say but also *how* you say it. Whether the audience is a small group of clinicians or the entire staff of a huge medical center, a leader's messages must be consistent, clear, and well thought out, as well as connected to the organization's mission, vision, and values.

Micromessaging refers to how a message is tailored to a particular audience. When speaking to a small team or work group, for example, you may offer the same overarching message as you would to the entire establishment, but with a different nuance and texture. You'd address people by name, add humor (but only if you're actually good at it), and perhaps weave in stories and anecdotes about some of those present to ally yourself with the group and cultivate a feeling of intimacy.

That kind of intimacy is important. Even when conveying information about financial performance or sharing statistics on quality measures, you need—in healthcare especially—to connect your messages to the humans who keep the place humming and whose efforts in safety, quality, and compassion lie at the very heart of the organization's success. Many smart senior healthcare leaders aren't able to connect their messages to their stakeholders and therefore lose their audience's attention—and their esteem. Although you may be terrific at sharing news about, say, a budget turnaround, if you fail to mention what's at the core of it—the people—you're sure to lose your colleagues' loyalty and to tarnish your reputation. Employees, physicians, nurses, and board members all want to know that their leader understands the connection between their decisions and outcomes and the organization's mission, vision, and values. Some people are so good at such messaging that they achieve lofty career heights even without positive statistical trends to back them.

As a nurse leader, you can learn to manage your messaging more effectively through simple planning and practice. Here are some tips:

- **Choose the medium.** The most persuasive messages are delivered in person. Telephone, e-mail, and text messages are increasingly less persuasive ways to communicate and often result in misunderstandings of tone, aim, and content.
- **Master your delivery.** How you say it is just as important as what you say. Although you don't have to be a stage performer to be a good speaker, your personal commitment and passion about the subject matter should sing through your message. Speak with authority, clarity, and confidence. Be eloquent, but use sufficiently plain language to ensure you're understood. Use voice tone, inflection, and pitch to your advantage, and enunciate clearly and use enough pauses to ensure your audience stays with you, particularly if you're sharing dense information.
- **Tell the truth.** People appreciate being leveled with, so if you're sharing bad news, be up front, factual, and

frank about it and then move on to solutions. Keep your messages congruent with your values. If you compromise your core beliefs to manipulate an outcome, others will pick up on your insincerity.

- **Be brief.** Group key points into buckets. If your purpose is to share information, offer facts with an anecdote illustrating each point so that it's more easily remembered. Keep your buckets to a maximum of three.

- **Avoid jargon.** Don't overuse acronyms, medical-speak, or technical jargon. Use simple words and simple sentences, but without being overly casual. Don't address your audience as "you guys" or talk the way you did in college; keep your words professional.

- **Monitor your body language.** Keep your facial expression in sync with the tone and content of your message. Bad news should not be delivered with a smirk or smile, and good tidings should not be accompanied by a sour or expressionless face. Especially if your message is being recorded, your gestures should be confined to the area near your waist and not distract from your face. Your gaze should be steady but not staring.

- **Know your talking points.** Don't lose your message in the medium or dart off down tangential rabbit trails at the slightest provocation. Stay on point. Be consistent and convincing in your position, state it firmly and clearly, and know when to stop. News reporters will take advantage if they sense you're waffling or easily distracted.

- **Know your audience.** Although your talking points may essentially be the same whether you're addressing a large group or a small one, you should customize your message to the audience. Put yourself in their place. What are their particular concerns about or interests in the topic? If you're talking about your new accountable care organization, for example, you'd address an audience of physicians differently than you would a board of directors or community forum. Be respectful of people's time and understanding—tailor what you say.

- **Understand you'll have critics.** Some people will take what you say out of context and attempt to use your message against you. Don't let these individuals fluster or anger you; manage the situation by remembering your main points and refusing to engage in tangential discussions that put you on the defensive. Know when to stop talking, and if questions persist, say firmly, "I believe I've answered your question. I don't think I can say more. Let's move on."

As a nurse leader, you'll need to communicate regularly with your key stakeholders about the organization's health, the issues it faces, its progress on overarching goals, and any major decisions that will affect everyone. Although you will share similar messages over and over, with the same talking points, remember that the information is brand new to many people—so treat every message as though you're giving your talk for the first time. Even if you feel you're "hypercommunicating," your message will be well received if it is well thought out and delivered succinctly, truthfully, and in an organized fashion.

EXERCISE 1

If proper messaging is holding back your career, hire a communications coach.

EXERCISE 2

The camera provides the best feedback, so ask a reporter or journalist to help you practice being interviewed in front of a camera.

You might also take a media training class or enroll in a continuing education program to help you improve your communication skills.

RESOURCES

Fink, S. 2013. *Crisis Communications: The Definitive Guide to Managing the Message.* New York: McGraw-Hill Education.

Young, S. 2006. *Micromessaging: Why Great Leadership Is Beyond Words.* New York: McGraw-Hill.

Raise Your Hand to Volunteer

Mahatma Gandhi said, "Be the change that you wish to see in the world." This powerful advice has always been deeply meaningful to me because it represents the great value of active volunteering. Not only does volunteering give us the opportunity to advance an important cause; it also gives us a deeper insight into who we are as people and as leaders. That level of awareness is what defines us as leaders, allows us to be instruments of change, and brings out the best in those whom we serve.

—Cathy D. Catrambone, PhD, RN, FAAN, associate professor, Rush University College of Nursing, Chicago, Illinois, and president (2015–2017), Sigma Theta Tau International, Honor Society of Nursing

IMAGINE IT: YOUR boss says at a management meeting, "We need volunteers to work on a performance improvement team to improve patient flow in the emergency department." Patient flow is not your area of expertise, you're a nurse manager of an inpatient unit, and you're not at all familiar with the people who work in the emergency department. So what do you do?

Raise your hand!

Volunteering for projects in your organization or for professional organizations such as Sigma Theta Tau International can help you learn new skills and allow you to interface with a whole new group of colleagues you may not otherwise meet. And if you develop a reputation as someone who can identify problems and solutions and work hard to get things done outside the confines of your job description, you'll not only be appreciated—you'll also be noticed.

Why volunteer?

- **Volunteering allows you to advocate for patients, nurses, and healthier communities.** Nurses need to have a place at the table when decisions are being made about healthcare delivery and policy. That's why, in 2014, the American Nurses Association and the American Academy of Nursing founded the Nurses on Boards Coalition—a campaign whose goal is to place 10,000 nurses on governing boards by 2020.

- **Volunteering exposes you to new areas of your organization.** Nurse leaders often find themselves in jobs that are confined to one unit or to a geographic area of work, and they may think that tasks that fall outside the parameters of their job description can't be touched. On the contrary, expanding your knowledge and network by working across departmental and professional boundaries is immensely useful.

- **Volunteering expands your vantage.** Volunteering is a great way to understand the larger issues confronting your organization and profession. Working on organization-wide projects and initiatives will also help you see how everything is interrelated. With this knowledge, you will be better prepared to take on jobs with more responsibility in the future.

- **Volunteering is a great way to network and meet new people.** Working outside your usual domain allows you to meet new people. Establishing a far-reaching network is a good way to solve problems and to tap broad resources when you tackle issues down the road. It can also

introduce you to distant allies who may be able to help
you bypass more cumbersome routes to quickly obtain the
information or results you're after.

- **Volunteering helps you grow your gifts and develop
  new skills.** Want to develop stronger leadership skills?
  Volunteer to be an officer of a social or volunteer
  organization such as Habitat for Humanity or United
  Way. Not only will you develop a wide variety of contacts
  outside your company, but you'll also have a chance to
  interface professionally with other like-minded individuals
  and to hone your skills as a speaker, a professional, and a
  go-to person. And besides advancing the common good,
  you'll spread the message that such values are important to
  you and your organization.
- **Volunteering will earn you a reputation as someone
  who gets things done and isn't afraid of work.** Show
  you're not too big a snob to roll up your sleeves and pitch
  in. Develop a personal brand as someone who can work on
  a project and get effective results, someone who can take a
  problem—however big or small—and solve it. Don't shirk
  from menial tasks, should they come up—get in there and
  tackle them with grace, good humor, and respect for those
  who do such tasks every day.

And don't always wait to be asked to help. Step up!

Perhaps your organization is struggling with declining revenue
and volume, a problem you've been mulling over. At a leaders'
meeting at which the problem is being discussed, you might say, "I
think we should consider working more closely with our physicians
to find out how we can make it easier for them to bring patients to
our hospital." You might go on to share, "Several physicians and
patients have recently mentioned to me the difficulties they face when
trying to schedule procedures at our outpatient center. I'd love the
chance to lead a team to look into this problem, to see if there's a
solution that would help grow our hospital's volume."

Would you like to learn more about your organization's information technology systems? Volunteer to become your department's representative on the information technology committee to represent nursing, or ask to be included in its system users' group. With a little effort, you can become the go-to person when computer problems arise. This is an example of identifying a problem and generating your own role in helping solve it, for both yourself and others.

Is your organization raising money for a local charity? Participating in fund-raising efforts is an excellent way to meet people in your organization over a good cause. Holiday charity drives for food, toys, or financial assistance are a great way to help, show leadership, and join your colleagues in togetherness.

If your employer does not offer opportunities for strengthening your financial skills, consider becoming the treasurer of a local charity to achieve that goal. Basic accounting functions are much the same from organization to organization, and you'll be able to better understand the healthcare business by working on real problems in real organizations.

As a nurse, you will always have many opportunities to volunteer—both within your organization and for professional organizations or your community. Nurses need to have a place at the table to advocate for patients, communities, and nursing as a profession. Don't be that reluctant leader who fails to step up when volunteers are needed. If you work hard and share your talents with the people, organizations, and communities that need them, you will make a difference.

EXERCISE 1

Identify a social service organization that personally interests you, and ask the staff there how you might be of service. Volunteer your time for a single day or for a single project—such as United Way's Day of Caring—or offer your skills as part of a committee or on a more regular basis. Keep a journal to help you comprehend and maximize the value of the project to your career development, maintaining a running tally of your contributions. Remember to thank the organizer of your project for allowing you to contribute.

EXERCISE 2

Think about the nursing organizations of which you're a member. How can you get more involved as a volunteer? Consider joining a committee, running for an elected position, or helping out at a social function. List the benefits of serving in capacities in which you can make a difference.

RESOURCES

Corporation for National & Community Service. 2017. "About Us." Accessed February 9. www.nationalservice.gov.

Hassmiller, S., and J. Combes. 2012. "Nurse Leaders in the Board-room: A Fitting Choice." *Journal of Healthcare Management* 57 (1): 8–11.

VolunteerMatch. 2017. "Where Volunteering Begins." Accessed February 9. www.volunteermatch.org.

Welcome a Multigenerational Workforce

Having been in leadership positions for a number of years, I was away from hands-on critical care for longer than I would have liked. On one deployment to Iraq, we were critically short of ICU nurses, and I was asked (as a Major) to cover some shifts as "the most experienced ICU nurse in northern Iraq." I found myself taking care of a soldier on a type of ventilator that didn't even exist when I was actively working in critical care. This wasn't the time or place to "fake it until you make it," so I decided to ask for help from a very junior and much younger ICU nurse on the unit. This decision resulted in a strong and fruitful mentoring relationship, and all the other nurses heard that the "Major" respected and sought input from the younger nurses. Ego is not a language any generation speaks.

—Col. Timothy Hudson, PhD, RN, FACHE, chief nursing officer, Evans Army Community Hospital, Fort Carson, Colorado

THE LOGICAL CONSEQUENCE of Americans living and working longer than ever before reveals itself in the mix of ages in any given workplace. Baby boomers, gen Xers, millennials, and now postmillennials arrive at their jobs informed by a variety of experiences, expectations, and interpersonal styles—and with effort all around, they can work together seamlessly, respectfully, and harmoniously. But that tone of respect is set by their leader. When leaders learn to see and appreciate the value in everyone present, whether they are of the same generation or not, they bring out the best in people and enable the team to perform well, thoughtfully, and cohesively.

Here are a few pointers for those who work with colleagues of different ages and from a variety of backgrounds (which, frankly, is pretty much all of us):

- **Learn to accept help wherever you find it.** Those just starting out sometimes think they have all the answers. But with age and growing wisdom and experience comes an often gradual realization that we *all* need help and can't go it alone. One sign of a confident, competent leader is the ability to listen to advice from *all* who wish to give it, whether they're older, younger, less educated, more senior, or otherwise. You will begin to grow as a leader when you realize that you do not have all the answers and you start seeking advice from your colleagues—and not just your top brass—and listen earnestly to what they say. Two (or three or four) are better than one.

- **Expand beyond your peers.** Be open to and friendly with everyone on your team—not just those whom you'd prefer to have lunch with or who are more in line with your age, political views, or social class. Exchange pleasantries and chitchat with *all* team members, making sure never to play favorites or to be cliquish such that some people or groups feel excluded.

- **Respect your elders.** Do you cringe when you hear, "Back in *my* day, it wasn't so easy. We had to. . . ."? Cringe-worthy or not, all employees—especially older workers who have been around longer—deserve to be listened to and have their points of view respected. Health systems have changed dramatically in recent years, and these individuals climbed the ranks in a different world where progression up the career ladder was more predictable and took place over the course of years. Respect their contributions and history, and understand that the job you have today exists because of past structures and the support and contributions of earlier generations.

- **Support work–life balance.** Everyone approaches this issue differently. Some expect their jobs to finish at 5:00 p.m. and not resume until 9:00 a.m. the next day, no matter the circumstance or time of year, whereas others are in constant contact by phone, e-mail, or text messaging. Whatever the viewpoint, drive your employees fairly while they're on task in the office, keeping your expectations high but manageable, and be respectful of their off-hours when they take lunch or leave for the day. Not everyone is driven by a 24/7 mentality of über-connectedness, and some may resent the implication that they're slacking off if they're not constantly accessible.

- **Ditch the notion of a perfect job, employee, or organization.** Young workers with limited work experience (other than an internship or two) often expect products to be flawless and processes to always make sense. Not only are such expectations unrealistic, but they're also untenable—and they can be irritating or degrading to other, more seasoned employees who have seen people come and go. Don't expect perfection, and know that the jobs you do won't be perfect, either—and that's fine. With time and experience, you'll understand that *all* jobs and companies have problems that may be exasperating if they're not addressed efficiently. You'll learn a great deal about the healthcare business if you stay and work through problems rather than throw your hands up in frustration every time you run into an obstacle.

- **Be realistic about your abilities.** Just because you received a master's degree from a prestigious university doesn't mean you have all the answers. Many of the best nurse leaders got their skills from real-world experiences— not textbooks—as well as through a lot of listening and collaborating with others. If a solution seems easy to you, you'd be wise to discuss it with some of your older colleagues first because it has likely been attempted before. You may learn some valuable information or history about the organization that will inform the answers you propose so that they'll *really* work—because they're guided by a longer-term perspective.

- **Have realistic expectations.** While it's invigorating to dream about a Mark Zuckerberg brand of near-instant success, such achievements are exceedingly rare. Most of us have to pay our dues in terms of education and experience to make progress in our careers. So although you likely won't swoop in and improve patient care, increase nurse retention, and dramatically boost your hospital's bottom line all in the first six months through your own brand of personal dynamism, you will find that slow, steady, meaningful progress is within your reach if you work hard, include others, and set reasonable expectations for yourself. Having a realistic view of the healthcare world, your abilities, and the manner in which you will climb the leadership ladder is essential.

- **Don't be a job hopper.** Think about your brand *before* you decide to change jobs. If you switch jobs or industries every year or two, how will it look on your resume? Gaps or quick moves from position to position can make you look flighty, unfocused, and unreliable. Appearing to be a job hopper is not to your advantage, and during interviews you may be asked to explain it. How long you stay at a place matters. Plan to stay at every job for at least five years. Give every job your best shot, and if it's not a good fit, make sure you're leaving for something better and for the right reasons. If you change positions every time you're confronted with a problem, experience conflict with a coworker, or find your interest and attention wilting, refocus yourself with purpose. Those who stay on to tackle difficult problems—and such problems exist in every job—will glean far more than will those who skedaddle every time the going gets tough.

EXERCISE 1

Invite a colleague of a different generation to lunch or coffee. Ask her opinion about how to proceed with some of the problems you're encountering, and show that you value her insight.

EXERCISE 2

When tackling your next problem or project, seek advice and counsel from a wider group of people than you would normally use—perhaps double the usual number. Try tapping staff other than the usual suspects and include people of varying ages. See what comes of this experiment, and take note of any staff strengths you hadn't anticipated.

RESOURCES

Jones, A. L. 2016. *Nurse Commitment: How to Retain Professional Staff Nurses in a Multigenerational Workforce.* Montgomery, AL: Visionary Consulting Services.

Taylor, P., and Pew Research Center. 2014. *The Next America: Boomers, Millennials, and the Looming Generational Showdown.* New York: PublicAffairs.

Manage Your Boss

One of the greatest lessons I ever learned was how important it is to manage my boss. Well along in a successful career, in my third chief-of-nursing role, I abruptly discovered I needed to be better at "managing up." Our organization had embarked on a 360-degree assessment of all executives, and I was rated exemplary by everyone but one person: my boss. The experience helped me understand that my autonomous style wasn't enough—I needed to keep my boss informed, share vision and goals, and develop effective two-way communication. Today, I use what I learned to coach new leaders. And although it sounds simple, it is communication basics that most often get in the way of success.

—Shirley R. Gibson, DNP, MSHA, RN, FACHE,
associate vice president of support services,
Virginia Commonwealth University Health System, Richmond

BOSSES COME IN all varieties, from overbearing to absent, intrusive to inspiring—and in most cases, you can't control that. But you *can* control how competent, cooperative, reliable, and honest *you* are. You depend on your boss to give you what you need to work well and to explain how you are connected to the larger purpose and goals of your organization. You both need a relationship that is built on mutual respect and regular communication. And a prerequisite is having a realistic view of each other's abilities, weaknesses, implicit and explicit goals, work styles, and needs—all informed by an ongoing level of respect and openness.

The most important work relationship for you to manage is the one with your boss. If you're not working hard at it, you're likely not as motivated or engaged as you should be. Managing your boss well—and being manageable yourself—enables you to do your best, to identify and own your success, and to benefit yourself and your organization in the process.

As the employee, you must learn how your boss processes information and makes decisions, what she expects from you, and how best to negotiate priorities. What works with one boss may not work with another, so early on in your job you should assess how the two of you can work together to manage expectations, understand your roles and responsibilities, and maximize results. Figure out which ways you'll be best heard—and which tactics will get you a vacant, glassy-eyed stare as you talk. Employee–boss relationships can be maddening, but by offering your best work and showing a dogged determination to respectfully connect and engage, you'll be doing your part to build a successful relationship.

It is, however, a two-way street, and a successful working relationship can mean great results. One boss—we'll call her Anne—was brought in to take over a newly restructured division of nursing at a large university hospital. Although Anne had significant experience in critical care—she had served as a nurse manager and director of critical care nursing prior to her arrival—she lacked experience with large, unwieldy academic medical centers. And despite her competence in critical care nursing management, she lacked hands-on experience with complex organizational operations that included other kinds of nursing as well as non-nursing-related operations. However, Anne's second-in-command had what she didn't have, and together they complemented one another beautifully. Both were open about their individual strengths and deficits, and both routinely reminded their staff that they depended on each another—and their larger team—to achieve the kind of results that were win–win all around.

To cultivate a strong, respectful relationship with your boss, keep these ideas in mind:

- **Know what your boss expects.** Managing expectations is key to knowing how to focus your time and energy. Without clarity, you and your supervisor may be working out of sync. Always ask, clarify, and check in. You might ask, "What does 'good' look like on this project?" or "If this went exactly the way you wanted it to go, turning out perfectly, what would happen between now and the end of the project?" It is your job to coax these important answers out of your boss, especially if he doesn't offer explanations first, or freely. Clarify your role by questioning, checking in, and then repeating those steps until the project is completed.

- **Understand your boss's perspective and adjust your approach.** Business guru Peter Drucker notes two key leadership communication styles: readers and listeners. Study your boss's style, determine whether she prefers to receive information orally or in print, and tailor your communications accordingly. Also, determine whether your boss takes the long view or immediately jumps on the available facts.

- **Provide information at your boss's comfort level.** Although you are not a mind reader, you may sometimes have to guess what your boss needs or wants. Your boss may forget to tell you details that could save you time. Take the initiative to learn as much as you can about every new project you're assigned. Be up front about deadlines, resources, and point people at a project's outset. If a project isn't going as expected, let your boss know, and don't sugarcoat issues to please because your boss wants honesty. Always consider timing, which affects one's ability to be heard. Don't approach your boss to discuss a problem when he is preoccupied, stressed, or working under a tight deadline. If you're tuned in to him, you'll know when the right time is.

- **Be open if there has been a miscommunication.** Your boss is in charge, but that doesn't mean that you should be a yes-man. If you disagree with your boss, say so—but do it respectfully and be prepared to back up what you say with facts and a well-rehearsed (and firm but gentle) argument. Begin your statements with "I think" or "I feel" so that you own your points of view and feelings. For example, after an uncomfortable or confrontational dialogue, you might say, "I need to check in with you about our conversation yesterday. When you expressed what you did, I felt hurt and upset. Is that what you meant? Did I misunderstand?" It's up to you to say you don't fully understand what transpired. Similarly, it's your responsibility to speak up when you feel or think you haven't been heard.

- **Respect your boss's position.** If you have bad news to impart, tell your boss first—no surprises and no undermining her in front of others. When you present a problem, be prepared to offer solutions rather than making your boss shoulder it entirely. On a practical level, when you're new, don't regularly arrive later than or leave before your boss does. You want not only to be accessible and open to dialogue in those early days but also to show that you're working hard and to the best of your ability—and that you're around and able to help.

- **Seek feedback on your performance.** Although you don't want to seem "high maintenance" or constantly self-centered, asking your boss for occasional feedback is important as you settle into a position. If your boss offers only positive feedback, it's up to you to dig in a little, asking for ways your boss thinks you might improve or for opportunities to take on more responsibilities than you currently have. Seek criticism and coaching in your areas of deficit. Help your boss prepare for your annual review by compiling a list of your accomplishments, a self-assessment, and other information. Accept and appreciate criticism without defensiveness, and be grateful for opportunities to improve.

In some situations in professional life, the employee–boss relationship sours and doesn't appear easily fixable. When it's not going well, your boss holds the key to your short-term future in that he can release you at any time—a terrifying position to be in, in any economy. Some bosses may unconsciously marginalize their employees by not communicating or by giving desirable projects to and allying themselves with others. If you sense that something has shifted in your relationship with your boss or that communication is dropping off, take it as a sign to either sort things out or move on (see lessons 49 and 50). Don't depart in an emotional flounce or with a dramatic exit, however. If you move on to another post, analyze how you might have better managed your boss—and then, when you're employed again, do things differently so that it doesn't happen again.

EXERCISE 1

Think about a time when things didn't go well with your boss. How could you have managed the situation differently? What personal values or approaches were in conflict? What did you learn from that experience that you will carry forward?

EXERCISE 2

When a situation with your boss doesn't go as you had planned and you have lingering hurt or angry feelings, rather than send the unpleasantness to a compartment deep inside, take charge of it. How can you address the situation in a follow-up conversation without sounding defensive or apologizing for your viewpoint? Write about this experience in your journal.

RESOURCE

Gabarro, J. J., and J. Kotter. 2008. *Managing Your Boss*. Boston: Harvard Business Review Press.

Engage and Partner with Physicians

Nurse leaders and physicians must work together for the good of the patients and communities they serve. While a shared mission and great communication are required, the two groups don't always understand words and concepts the same way. For example, physicians may think patient advocacy means advocating only for their patients, whereas nurses might use the same term to describe the greater good for an entire unit, hospital, or community. These two "advocacies" may thus clash—for example, when making decisions about allocating scarce resources. To work together, doctors and nurses must first acknowledge their differing professional cultures and then seek to understand each other's perspective.

—Kathleen Sanford, DBA, RN, FACHE, FAAN,
senior vice president and chief nursing officer,
Catholic Health Initiatives, Denver

PHYSICIAN–NURSE ADMINISTRATOR relationships are often cast as asymmetric dyads, with different power bases and goals. But why? Perhaps strong professional boundaries, confusing payment structures, different incentives, and poorly aligned processes cause the divide.

However, the two groups are basically in sync. Physicians and nurses want the best possible care for their patients. And although administrators are necessarily more wedded to the organization's bottom line, they want exactly the same thing. So acknowledging at the outset that your goals align is a positive place to begin.

How well you work with physicians is an important predictor of how successful you'll be as a nurse administrator and leader. If you can forge strong, honest, and respectful relationships with physicians, you will gain a reputation as someone who is capable of developing close personal and professional bonds—and thereby increase your career potential immensely.

When you engage and align yourself with physicians, you establish partnerships that make for the best patient care possible. So how do you do that?

- **Understand what physicians want.** Nurse leaders should view problems from the physicians' vantage as well as their own and come up with solutions that give a nod to both sides. If you don't know what physicians want, ask. Be clear about what's at stake, and listen. Make sure decisions aren't of the winner-take-all variety—meet in the middle so that both sides get something they want and no one feels they got the short end of the stick.
- **Build relationships.** Get to know your physicians. Ask them to describe the problems they face, and then help them find routes to meaningful and permanent solutions. Be the first to offer support for an issue, and grant favors that are within your power, big and small. Be a servant leader—someone who makes it easier for doctors to do their job. At the same time, be humble about it. Your ethic and efforts will be valued, remembered, and likely returned in kind.
- **Stand tall in your own skin while still maintaining humility.** Don't be fearful, intimidated, or starstruck by physicians' knowledge, power, or multiple academic degrees; they are human beings with pasts, wishes, fears, and goals just like you. Dealing comfortably with smart,

successful physicians is crucial to your career as a nurse manager or executive. Remember, their role is different but not necessarily more important. So be confident in your dealings with physicians. Like anyone, physicians can smell intimidation and may use it to their advantage—or as an excuse not to take you seriously.

- **Respect doctors' time constraints.** Doctors and healthcare executives often work in different time zones when it comes to decision making. Physicians need information to diagnose and treat their patients and often make decisions on the spot with the data they have. Thus, a physician may make numerous decisions about multiple patients in the same 30-minute visit to a patient floor. Healthcare executives, on the other hand, need to get input and buy-in from others and must spend time investigating problems and researching apt solutions before solidifying their decision. For example, an administrator may spend many months working on next year's budget. So remember doctors' time constraints, and give them the information they need as promptly as possible.
- **Be flexible.** It's the nature of the beast: Physicians have chaotic, intensely busy days with back-to-back patients, and they may not be able to stop by your office. Therefore, go where they are: Be available when they have some downtime between surgeries, meet them in the doctors' lounge, or stop by their office after their last patient of the day. Don't make a big deal about bending over backward—simply anticipate that you'll need to accommodate them.
- **Speak respectfully to and about your physician colleagues.** Never complain about physicians to anyone, and never engage in conflict with a doctor in public. Your physician colleagues must feel that you are trustworthy

and respectful and that you value them, their role, and their work. Expect the same of them.

- **Do your best to involve physicians in decisions and plans.** Often, physicians are brought in at the last minute to approve a new piece of equipment, lend support for a new program, or confirm a forthcoming policy change. They're busy, of course. But although they may not be able to attend meetings or thoroughly read the material you send to them, they do likely want to be involved in decisions that affect their work. Figure out how to include them in your organization's processes and decisions early on so that there's no scramble for support when decision time comes.

- **Identify and ally yourself with informal physician leaders.** A few physicians have powerful medical and social influence, as well as the intense respect of their colleagues. Although it may not be readily apparent early on in your tenure who these individuals are—particularly given that many thought leaders aren't necessarily the most vocal— do your best to seek them out and establish rapport and trust with them.

- **Be consistent in your messages.** Sometimes a nurse manager or executive says no to a physician, and the physician then appeals to the CEO, who reverses the decision. Not only does this kind of sequence disempower the original manager, but it also undermines respect for other managers and sends the message to physicians that the administrative team lacks consensus. Unless you are confident that your response will be supported by executive leadership, limit your authority before saying yes or no to a physician's request by saying that you need to check with others who know more about the issue than you do.

- **Reward and recognize.** Physicians offer a great deal of themselves, their time, and their energy to patient care and service. And although they enjoy a certain degree of glory for what they do, they still like to be thanked. Leaders can recognize physicians' commitment in both financial and nonmonetary ways, but remember that a meaningful thank-you note is perhaps the most effective and memorable way to personalize your appreciation.

Throughout your career, learn as much as you can about your physician colleagues, both personally and professionally. Contrary to popular assumption, nurses and doctors don't always understand how the other group was educated or their corresponding scope of practice. To help avoid misconceptions about each other and to develop meaningful relationships, spend time accompanying doctors on rounds—and express genuine curiosity about what they do and face daily.

Remember, you're both there for the same reason: to do what's best for the patient.

EXERCISE 1

Spend time with physicians. Learn more about their viewpoints—specifically, how their work could be streamlined administratively. Ask to accompany them in the operating room or on rounds.

EXERCISE 2

If you have a physician leader counterpart in your area of responsibility, attend a continuing education program with that person to fine-tune your dyad leadership potential.

RESOURCES

Bujak, J. S. 2008. *Inside the Physician Mind: Finding Common Ground with Doctors*. Chicago: Health Administration Press.

Fields, R. 2011. "7 Reasons Hospitals Struggle to Align with Physicians." *Becker's Hospital Review*. Published July 29. www .beckershospitalreview.com/hospital-physician-relationships /7-reasons-hospitals-struggle-to-align-with-physicians.html.

Sanford, K., and S. Moore. 2015. *Dyad Leadership in Healthcare: When One Plus One Is Greater Than Two*. Philadelphia, PA: Lippincott Williams & Wilkins.

Build Strong Teams

Nurses learn very little about doctors in nursing school, and doctors learn very little about nurses in medical school. In the hospital, we come together from this position of relative ignorance and are expected to work closely, often on matters of life and death. Why anyone thinks that's a good strategy for effective healthcare is a mystery to me.

—Theresa Brown, PhD, BSN, RN, clinical nurse
and author of the *New York Times* bestseller
The Shift: One Nurse, Twelve Hours, Four Patients' Lives

IMAGINE FOR A moment all the special knowledge it takes to perform open-heart surgery, a procedure in which many professionals work together in an elaborately choreographed production to ensure a patient receives the best, most thorough care possible. We take it for granted that strong, communicative, interdisciplinary teams just happen. But the truth is that collaborative teams are usually carefully cultivated.

Twenty-first-century healthcare delivery is a team business. We may rotate in and out of teams several times every day, working across professional lines, adroitly moving among physical environments, varying our roles, and collaborating with a range of experts. That is the nature of healthcare and the nature of seamless, coordinated delivery.

The airline industry has long understood the criticality of collaboration and spends a great deal of time and energy training its employees to be effective team members. Healthcare is increasingly coming to understand that it, too, must follow the airlines' example, investing in interprofessional training so that, ultimately, the patient, clinician, and organization all benefit.

Whether from coursework or ancillary reading, most healthcare leaders are familiar with the concept of high-reliability organizations. These organizations—in industries such as healthcare and aviation—must rely on teamwork for synchronicity, anticipation, real-time adjustments, deference to expertise, and knowing what to do quickly when things go awry. If you are that patient on the operating room table or a passenger 30,000 feet in the air during a crisis, you hope there is a team that knows what to do (and has practiced its moves) should an emergency take place. The key point here is that a high-performing team can make all the difference in the world in terms of outcome.

Members of high-performing teams must have a great degree of trust in one another. Airline crews are frequently different for each flight, and although they may not know their peers intimately, they share a job and goal—the safety of passengers—that informs their every move. As you progress in your career, the way you champion teamwork will be crucial to your—and your organization's—success.

To develop and support strong interprofessional teams, you should do the following:

- **Dedicate resources to initial and ongoing teamwork training.** Teams don't just materialize out of thin air. They're nurtured, trained in what makes a good team, and taught the technical skills required to act nimbly when unanticipated events occur.
- **Get the right people on the team.** Mix it up. If yours is a performance improvement team, for example, add a financial analyst to solve problems related to patient

throughput. Varied perspectives add richness and will fortify a more robust response.

- **Encourage interprofessional education and collaboration.** Clinical improvement teams need to be supported with training, resources, and tools. If your nurses and therapists are not involved in patient rounds every day, they must begin immediately. If you work in a teaching hospital with medical and nursing students, champion education across professional boundaries. If your organization is not an academic medical center, you can still get nurses and doctors together for continuing education. Talk it up, offer readings and resources, and let your platform be that working well together really matters.

- **Train for leadership and followership.** Your role on the team may change as needs and members shift. One day you may be the leader and the next a follower—and that's okay. Learn that your role as a leader may sometimes be to follow in lockstep with your colleagues behind someone else's instruction. Too many leaders can result in inefficiency and can be a recipe for disaster.

- **Create checklists, but don't be a slave to them.** Such tools are good for quality purposes and help ensure that the steps taken are evidence based to yield positive outcomes. However, checklists followed mindlessly may lead to problems. So pay attention to the qualitative aspects of the tasks at hand. If the patient or problem doesn't fit neatly into a checklist, then use your professional judgment—and the expertise of your team—to make an exception and find a better pathway.

- **Fix systems and processes to support teams.** If nurses are not rounding with doctors every day because each patient has a different doctor and doctors complain that they have to visit a dozen different units to see their patients, fix the issue. Your job as a manager is to do the behind-the-scenes organizational and administrative work so that the caregiving teams can concentrate on patient care, not worry about logistical details.

- **Make sure each team member understands and respects the other team members' jobs.** Synchronicity can occur only when team members are both competent and in firm agreement that their team is most effective working as a whole rather than individually.
- **Offer meaningful recognition.** High-performing teams receive intrinsic rewards from the positive outcomes of their interventions—the satisfaction of a job well done, for example. As a manager, however, know which teams of yours are outstanding and give recognition that is meaningful. In other words, share direct quotes from patients and families, physicians, and other colleagues, and praise the teams as exemplars of your organization's values. You don't need to wait until an extraordinary event takes place to do this; you can recognize teams that work together well every day, acknowledging that their work is critical and prevents medical errors.

Excellent teamwork can be also described as group or organizational mindfulness because teams must be in the moment, work together, and anticipate a full range of next steps. They must pick up on subtle cues, tap their vast reservoirs of nursing and medical knowledge, and, above all, communicate with one another.

But interprofessional agility isn't experienced only in the hospital; it can also take place in the boardroom. Notice people's body language and tone of voice, and be prepared to take your proposal or discussion in a different direction, if necessary, to ensure you're working together with your colleagues in the best manner possible.

Teams truly are at the center of providing care to patients and their families, and it is incumbent on you, the manager, to champion effective teamwork, provide resources to train teams, and recognize and reward their contributions. Working on a team that works together for the good of the patient is the greatest feeling in health-care. We hope that you have this experience!

EXERCISE 1

Ask one of your organization's high-performing interprofessional teams if you can shadow them to learn more about effective teamwork.

EXERCISE 2

Attend a teamwork training session, and put what you learn into practice. Many business schools offer such seminars and skills training workshops.

RESOURCES

Mosser, G., and J. W. Begun. 2013. *Understanding Teamwork in Health Care.* New York: McGraw-Hill Education.

Weiss, D., F. Tilin, and M. J. Morgan. 2013. *The Interprofessional Health Care Team: Leadership and Development.* Burlington, MA: Jones & Bartlett Learning.

Find and Fix Problems

*Every day we are responsible for the health, safety, and well-being
of thousands of patients who depend on us for safe care and positive
outcomes. At Bon Secours, we strive to implement a high-reliability
culture and processes that allow us to expect reliable outcomes 100
percent of the time. Achieving high reliability requires a culture that
sees safety and performance as top priorities and that promotes frequent
and constructive communication. When errors do occur, the entire
team takes part in finding solutions. Prepare for and achieve success
by embracing a desire to learn from failure.*

—Toni Ardabell, RN, MSN, MBA, chief executive officer,
Bon Secours Health System, Richmond, Virginia

THE MOST IMPORTANT skill for *any* manager in *any* field—
healthcare included—is the ability to recognize, define, and figure
out solutions to problems. Effective problem solvers will always have
career opportunities because of their ability to break down issues
and chart a path toward positive change.

The best way to learn to deal with issues is by working out *real*
problems in *real* organizations, big and small. But you have to start
somewhere. So seek assignments that allow you to tackle issues and
gain problem-solving experience. Volunteer, if necessary. Don't be
afraid of challenges, because you truly will learn by doing.

If you can, find out whether your company takes a formal or informal approach to problem solving. Many organizations use frameworks such as Lean and Six Sigma, and if your company is among them, become an expert in these techniques. Some organizations offer problem-solving training in-house, while others use local universities or other training facilities to hone their administrators' skills in analyzing issues. Certifications can be useful—the University of Michigan, for example, offers courses that lead to healthcare Lean and Six Sigma certification—so if a formal path is available to boost your problem-solving skills, make a case to attend.

Every problem is different, of course, but a systematic approach, such as the following, is prudent no matter what the issue is:

- **Recognize and define the problem.** This first step is often the most difficult. All too often, executives "solve" what they thought was the real problem only to discover that the problem persists after a great deal of attention, effort, and money has been spent on it. For example, a hospital that is suffering from declines in outpatient volume may think the root cause is a lack of branding. But even after a multimillion-dollar marketing and branding campaign, the problem of declining volumes might remain because the *real* problem was related to quality. As you define the problem, be honest—not hopeful. This is not the time to initiate an off-target pet project.
- **Focus on understanding the issue.** Hold frank discussions with both internal and external stakeholders to fully understand the parameters of the problem. Note every facet of the organization that the problem touches. Once the problem has been isolated, the solution will likely be straightforward.
- **Gather the *real* facts.** Everyone in the organization may think admissions are dropping because Dr. Jones is angry at the administrator or because Dr. Smith has a bad attitude and patients and staff find him difficult to work

with. Don't let yourself be distracted by false, superficial claims. Problems usually have simple, basic, and even obvious sources, and hurt feelings and office politics generally aren't at the root. Use Occam's razor—the principle that, of all possible solutions, the one involving the fewest assumptions is usually correct—to define what ails your organization. The simplest, most obvious, and most straightforward solution is likely the best answer.

- **Analyze the problem from all angles.** How much is the problem costing the organization? What are the potential benefits if it's solved? If feasible, capture the problem in numbers and narrative. Simplify it to its very essence. As the problem-solver-in-chief, you are responsible for presenting your findings succinctly. Keep your bullet points clear, clean, and concise. Develop a 60- to 90-second "elevator speech" about it for on-the-fly conversations and questions. Supporting information, research, and analysis should be close at hand for easy reference.

- **Talk it through, and listen well.** If you take time to listen to as many people as you can about a problem and how to solve it, a solution will crystallize. Know how to listen. Your chance to speak will come when you make a decision about a fix.

- **Share possible solutions with your constituents.** Engage in healthy discussions about solutions and their impacts. What are the pros and cons of each? As particular pathways out of the problem present themselves, get a sense of how people feel about each one. Consensus about a direction is key.

- **Decide on a course of action.** Do your best to ensure colleagues and stakeholders concur about which path to take. Expend extra effort to make sure practitioners embrace and follow changes. Involve both clinicians and nonclinicians in defining the problem and finding its solution.

- **Establish a metric and remain involved.** Monitor the issue carefully, charting the path to change until you see that progress has been achieved. Once a positive, preselected metric is reached and the problem appears to subside, assign follow-up efforts to a trusted colleague. Meet with that colleague regularly to ensure that progress in the right direction is being made.
- **Announce the successful completion of the project.** Let employees know when the measure is reached, and thank everyone for their support. Should the measure not be reached in the designated time frame, reconvene and chart a modified plan to accomplish the established metric of success.

Problem-solving skills are honed with practice, and your thoughtful study and analysis of problems will earn you praise and regard, as well as strengthen your ability to solve the next set of issues that crop up. The issues you successfully address will not only help your organization's bottom line but will also add a notch to your professional experience belt and prepare you for future roles.

EXERCISE 1

Keep a journal of the problems you have solved. What skills did you use? What worked and what didn't? Routinely study your journal to look for patterns that will help you hone your skills. Seek input and counsel from your supervisor.

EXERCISE 2

Find out as much as you can about the problem-solving method your organization uses. Study the problem-solving techniques of an organization you admire.

EXERCISE 3

Make a list of all of your projects. Is it clear who is responsible for each project's completion? Does the person responsible for completing each project have a level of authority that is commensurate with the project's scope of responsibility?

RESOURCES

Graban, M. 2012. *Lean Hospitals: Improving Quality, Patient Safety, and Employee Engagement*, 2nd ed. Boca Raton, FL: CRC Press.

Johns Hopkins Medicine Center for Innovation in Quality Patient Care. 2016. "What Is Lean Sigma?" Accessed July 18. www.hopkins medicine.org/innovation_quality_patient_care/areas_expertise /lean_sigma/about/.

University of Michigan College of Engineering. 2016. "Lean Healthcare: Combining World-Class Lean Healthcare Training Expertise with Hands-On Experience." Professional program. Accessed July 18. http://isd.engin.umich.edu/professional -programs/lean-healthcare/index.htm.

Be Visible by Rounding

*Excellence emanates at the point of care, and visibility matters.
Rounding provides leaders with an up-close and personal view of the
compassion, teamwork, and expertise of clinicians interacting with
patients. I am constantly astonished at what I learn when I round
in clinical areas. One palliative care team granted a teen's last wish
by organizing the transport and visitation of a pet horse on a winter
Sunday morning; another team in psychiatry executed complex
travel arrangements—involving multiple flights, assistance through
airport security, and a home inspection by a retired police officer—
for a patient with schizophrenia. By rounding, leaders can reinforce
organizational priorities, identify opportunities for improvement,
solve problems, and recognize those who matter most: clinicians
at the point of care.*

—Deb Zimmermann, DNP, RN, NEA-BC, FAAN,
chief nursing officer and vice president of patient care services,
Virginia Commonwealth University Health System, Richmond

SUCCESSFUL HEALTHCARE LEADERS know that being visible in
their organization is critical. The best healthcare leaders get out of
their offices, roam the halls and unit corridors, chat with employees,
and discover what's going on outside the confines of their usual
areas of responsibility. They're engaging, approachable, and curious,
and they listen well. Often, they're beloved simply because they're

seen, they care enough to take in the work of others, and they're not uncomfortable when outside the hallowed walls of the executive suite or when communicating with people who aren't wearing suits.

You could easily fill your calendar each day with meetings and calls and get caught up in daily activities that make you lose sight of *who* makes the organization hum and *how*. If you have an assistant, make sure you control your calendar and personally approve its entries. Be selective with your time so that you're able to fit in 30 to 60 minutes of rounds at least several times each week. Visibility is truly a key to executive success.

Rounding brings a bounty of benefits. It can be a great way to get buy-in from colleagues, to gather information about your company's culture, and to spread word about your ideas and initiatives. Executives who round show that they understand and appreciate their employees' hard work and dedication, and people will follow leaders who take the time to talk, listen, and explain their decisions. Although employees may not always agree with the leaders' decisions, they will respect their forthcoming attitude because they're there, in the trenches, taking the time to listen and learn.

The key to successful rounding is to do it regularly but not predictably. Make your approach at different times of day. Follow different routes, taking different corridors and elevators. Don't forget to visit places that aren't on the way to anywhere—offices in out-of-the-way corners, for example, or services that are off the beaten path or in remote locations. Round on weekend and holiday shifts, too, if you can. Offer special praise to those who work during off-hours. Ask people what they're working on and how it's going. And don't rush it. You'll be appreciated for your presence—and you'll have the opportunity to appreciate others.

Other aspects to successful rounding include the following:

- Address people by name, and introduce yourself to those you don't know.
- Express admiration for and curiosity about staffers' work and work strategies—and remember to thank them.

- Smile, be approachable, and be ready to talk to anyone who wishes to speak to you.
- If you see something exceptional or someone going beyond the call of duty, offer praise—and take note of it. Those who do good when no one's looking may be great people to tap for an award, promotion, or raise.
- If appropriate, and as time permits, use your rounds to ask physicians, employees, and patients for their opinions about any issues on your mind or theirs.
- Be respectful of the environment you're in. For example, if you're rounding in the intensive care unit or the emergency department, be sensitive in particular to the patients there as well as the tempo and stress levels of those caring for them.
- Remember to jot down notes so that, if you make a promise to do something, you'll remember to follow up. People always remember those who do what they say they're going to do because such behavior is rare. *Be that rare leader.*

A guiding principle for rounding—and for most of your interactions, save the most difficult ones—is the Golden Rule: Treat people the way you would like to be treated. Understand and believe that every contribution is important to your organization's proper and successful function. If someone is cleaning bathrooms, catch him with a smile, a handshake, and an honest, nonpatronizing compliment: "Your work is critical to our success and patient satisfaction. When I see the hospital looking good, I feel great—and so do our patients!"

Rounding also provides an opportunity to observe and curb lackluster or unprofessional behaviors. Look around you for opportunities for improvement, and jot a note to yourself to correct the problem or to follow up privately with the offender, if appropriate. If you see something out of order, inform the appropriate department leaders and give them a chance to correct it. Be on the lookout for opportunities to improve the work environment and make the area safer for patients. If you observe a situation that threatens the safety of patients or staff, take immediate corrective action.

Visiting all of the areas you're responsible for—and making appearances in areas where you're not in charge but that are integral to the organization's health—is one of the best ways to gather information and be an effective leader. Rounding truly represents the very best use of your time.

EXERCISE 1

Set a different goal as you round each day—something you can quantify. For example, one morning your goal might be to speak with five staff nurses. The next day, you could aim to speak with three physicians or two housekeepers. One day, try to visit three units that you haven't visited in a month.

EXERCISE 2

Make a point of meeting new people each day, and remember their names.

RESOURCES

Cleary, P. R., and J. S. Lindsey. 2013. "Navy Captain's Advice to the C-Suite: 5 Simple Leadership Tenets That Will Make Your Hospital Shine." *Becker's Hospital Review.* Published July 18. www.beckershospitalreview.com/white-papers/navy-captain-s -advice-to-the-c-suite-5-simple-leadership-tenets-that-will-make -your-hospital-shine.html.

Lindsey, J. S., and B. Corkran. 2012. "4 Keys to Effective Administrative Rounding." *Becker's Hospital Review.* Published May 22. www.beckershospitalreview.com/hospital-management -administration/4-keys-to-effective-administrative-rounding.html.

Recognize and Celebrate

*The tremendous impact that individual nurses have on patients and
families is demonstrated by the nearly one million stories submitted
as nominations for The DAISY Award for Extraordinary Nurses.
Yet nurses don't always see—in themselves or in others—the
unforgettable difference they make in the lives of their patients,
families, and coworkers.*

*From a simple "thank you" to formal recognition programs such as
The DAISY Award, frequent expressions of gratitude instill a culture
in which nurses understand the profound impact they have on others.
The power of gratitude reinforces the satisfaction nurses derive from
their compassionate work, providing the emotional energy they need
day in and day out. Given how hard their work is—physically,
mentally, and emotionally—nurses deserve nothing more than to
appreciate how deeply valued they are.*

—Bonnie Barnes, FAAN, and Mark Barnes, FAAN,
cofounders, The DAISY Foundation, Glen Ellen, California

ACCORDING TO THE American Association of Critical-Care
Nurses, six factors contribute to a healthy and successful work
environment (see lesson 45). One of those factors is *meaningful
recognition*—healthcare workers must "be recognized and recognize
others for the value each brings to the work of the organization."

Recognizing others in a meaningful way not only ensures a happy, engaged workforce but also improves patient satisfaction. And the human need for feeling valued by others, especially colleagues, is often ranked as more important than job security or pay increases. So how can we be better at responding to this very basic human need to belong, to be cherished, and to be respected for our contributions?

We often blame a perceived lack of time for our failure to properly offer thanks and praise to our colleagues. But in fact, recognition can feel tricky because you have to know the people you work with really well to know whether they prefer group or individual recognition. Rewarding teams, work units, and departments feels safer and easier because you don't risk embarrassing someone on the receiving end of praise. But just because it's hard or has the potential to make people feel awkward doesn't mean it should be skipped.

If you are mindful about praising yourself, rewarding others may come a bit more easily. The next time you finish a big task, spend some time soaking in the feeling of accomplishment before darting off to what's next. As you experience your own successes, be mindful of what has occurred and mark the occasion. Some teams have a fancy dinner out to celebrate accomplishments such as successfully implementing a new family visiting policy, opening a new service, publishing a journal article or book, or completing a successful accreditation site visit. Such rewards offer us time to reflect on what worked (and what didn't) and to set new goals for working together in the future.

Celebrations of accomplishments and of important events such as National Nurses Week or the anniversary of your organization's founding are all moments to mark what has been achieved, to offer reverence to a skill set, or to recognize why those around you are special. Although having *too* many parties may be unwise (moving from party to party can make you appear unsocial), simply acknowledging the need to recognize and celebrate is a great place to begin.

Here are some additional tips:

- **Catch people doing good.** When you see people going beyond what is expected for a patient or hear about a situation that reflects your organization's mission and values, recognize it personally and praise it publicly. Remember people's past contributions, too: "It was Bill's idea to try this in the pediatric intensive care unit—and look at the results!"
- **Reinforce outstanding performance in your messaging.** When you communicate with others, whatever the format, include positive stories about your associates—examples of excellent teamwork, devotion to and connection with the organization's mission, a good deed you spotted someone doing, or an anecdote about your organization's founder that humanizes, informs, and brings him closer to the mission and tone of the place.
- **Keep your praise specific.** "Good job!" loses its crispness of meaning if it's not tied to something specific. Instead, you might say, "I saw how you handled that challenging patient and family over the chaos of multiple admissions and discharges, and how you kept your cool. I'm impressed—and grateful." Name specific behaviors, such as compassion, patience, and cheerfulness in handling the specific needs of a patient or fellow nurse. Mention the strength to the person's supervisor, if that's not you. If your organization has formal programs for recognizing someone for doing good, take advantage of them by submitting a nomination whenever you see it's deserved. Also remember the world-class DAISY Awards that are offered each year to staff in participating hospitals.
- **Handwrite notes.** An e-mail will do the job, but it doesn't pack the same punch as a handwritten note. And although different generations may prefer different modes

of communication, a handwritten note is universally pleasing—and increasingly out of the ordinary.

- **Tune in to your network.** Be kind to your network contacts even when you don't need them. Offer praise routinely when you hear about their professional accomplishments. When a nurse you know gets a new job, earns an advanced degree, or achieves a certification credential, send her a note of congratulations. You can't go wrong with this kind of connection, and you never know when or why such gestures will be recalled.

- **Remember birthdays.** Keeping track of birthdays is far easier than you might imagine. Simply add your colleagues' birthdays to your e-mail calendar as a recurring event so that you are reminded a day or two in advance each year. Keep a stash of birthday cards in your desk drawer, call or e-mail your colleagues, or salute them in the hallway. As grownups, we don't put the same huge investment in birthdays as we did when we were kids, but it's fabulous when someone remembers ours.

- **Take team pictures, and post them.** Team photos reinforce how people in your organization are connected by a common purpose—and show they can have fun, too.

- **Be good at recalling names.** Remembering names is hard for many people. But once you start being mindful about it, recalling names—even hundreds or thousands of them—will come more easily to you. Just use a mnemonic or alliteration to connect the person's name to something that you will remember. Becky, for instance, is in charge of the building. And Olivia has round, O-shaped glasses.

- **Be inclusive.** In healthcare, much of the workforce works around the clock. Evening, night, and weekend staff may not get noticed the same way that the 9-to-5ers do. Show your appreciation for these staffers by arriving with pizza on the night shift or making rounds on a holiday. Word will travel like wildfire through the organization that you really care—and that you're willing to make the effort.

- **Exhibit compassion.** When things aren't going well and your staff are anxious, remember that they need to be cared for, too. Listen, console, and affirm. Don't focus all your attention on the superstars or dole out praise only when things are going swimmingly. Remember that many of your people are plugging away, day after day, doing their jobs without fanfare or reward, and that their jobs are critical to your organization's smooth operation. Find a way to thank everyone, including the facilities and housekeeping personnel, pharmacy staff, and patient care assistants. Acknowledge what they do, and recognize how they contribute.
- **Be thoughtful.** Send flowers to someone who starts a new job. When a major initiative is successfully completed or a major goal is achieved, host a lunch for the key organizers to let them know you've noticed them and their work.

All of us engaged in healthcare have a calling to serve people. We all want to know that our work is bigger than us and that it truly makes a difference. As leaders, we must practice recognizing others in meaningful ways and celebrating not only what they do at work but also who they are as people. In our profession, it *all* matters.

EXERCISE 1

Keep a list of events to celebrate and people to thank. Keep a stash of thank-you notes and birthday cards—and use them.

EXERCISE 2

Celebrate regularly with your staff, and engage them in developing a positive culture of celebration that is focused on helping people.

RESOURCES

American Association of Critical-Care Nurses. 2016. *AACN Standards for Establishing and Sustaining Healthy Work Environments: A Journey to Excellence*, 2nd ed. Aliso Viejo, CA: American Association of Critical-Care Nurses.

Barnes, B., M. Barnes, and C. D. Sweeney. 2016. "Supporting Recognition of Clinical Nurses with the DAISY Award." *Journal of Nursing Administration* 46 (4): 164–66.

DAISY Foundation. 2016. "What Is the DAISY Foundation?" Accessed July 28. www.daisyfoundation.org.

Kouzes, J. M., and B. Z. Posner. 2003. *Encouraging the Heart: A Leader's Guide to Rewarding and Recognizing Others*. San Francisco: Jossey-Bass.

Lefton, C. 2012. "Strengthening the Workforce Through Meaningful Recognition." *Nursing Economics* 30 (6): 331–38, 355.

Innovate

Many think about innovation, but only those who develop an innovative mind-set actually succeed at it. Asking yourself some key questions will help you understand what innovation is, and following practical advice will help you develop purposeful, innovative thinking. What will your innovation be?

—Jean Giddens, PhD, RN, FAAN, professor and dean, Doris B. Yingling Endowed Chair, School of Nursing, Virginia Commonwealth University, Richmond

INNOVATION IN HEALTHCARE reveals new and better ways to solve existing problems and overhaul complicated systems. Innovative leaders not only tackle issues in outside-the-box ways but also get things done—and get noticed. Although the "secret sauce" of innovation is made from a multi-ingredient recipe of perspective, planning, and approach, innovation itself is nothing more than taking existing ideas, technology, and procedures and reshaping them to produce a superior product; a better procedure; or novel, top-notch services. Innovators take old ideas and deploy them in new and better ways.

Of course, they have to be the right ideas—ones that are aligned with organizational goals and that have the potential to be flexible and replicable. And innovation usually involves change, sometimes of the 180-degree variety. But such change is necessary for organizations that want to get better, stronger, and more attuned to the marketplace so that they can ensure their relevancy to current and future environments. Particularly in a field as dynamic and ever-changing as healthcare, we can't simply do everything as we've always done it and expect to be at the top of our game. Change, in this profession in particular, is essential.

Apple Inc. is often cited as one of the most innovative companies of the past two decades. Founded by visionary Steve Jobs, Apple not only developed an interface that worked well for customers, but its platforms and products also brought technology to consumers in a whole new way: brilliantly designed, accessible, and user friendly. Before Apple, technology had never involved beautiful design, but Apple turned that notion on its head by making products that engaged humans on a very human level, appealing to them in very human ways. And how it worked!

Like computers in the era before Apple, healthcare is a field that is sorely overdue for beautiful, thoughtful, and creatively conceived ideas that truly serve the customer. As cumbersome as it has become—with layer upon layer of providers, laboratories, equipment, and countless billing offices—the industry has a host of parts that could be made better, more accessible, more user-friendly, and far more human. A scheduling system that allows patients to make appointments with their providers quickly and easily is one example of a system component that could be innovatively overhauled. Simplifying common nursing procedures or providing a way for patients to choose a primary care provider on the basis of reviews are other processes in dire need of an overhaul. A billing system that enables patients to see and understand their costs for any given procedure up front, according to the insurance they have and the procedures they anticipate having done, is another area that could use attention. You might consider what issue in your organization ensnares and maddens the most customers, clinicians, and others—and then move in to begin your own innovation.

So how can you make things move better and faster? Here are a few questions to consider at the outset:

- Thinking about your organization's current strengths, what new products or services spring to mind that would not involve a huge investment in capital?
- How might you rethink solutions to the problems your organization currently faces?
- What resources and individuals do you need to bring about the change you're eyeing?
- Who are your most forward-thinking colleagues, and can they help you devise innovative solutions to problems your organization faces?
- Are your target innovations in line with your organization's strategic goals and culture?
- Can you ally yourself with any external strategic partners and use your collective strengths to offer a new product or better service?
- Once your innovation is implemented, how and with whom will you need to communicate to ensure it becomes the "new normal"? How will you measure whether your innovation is working, and who is responsible for making it work?
- Is your innovation sustainable?

Robert Tucker's *Innovation Is Everybody's Business* offers seven ways to prepare for innovative opportunities:

1. **Consciously shift your perspective.** Think of problems as opportunities and brainstorm ways to fix them.
2. **Think small.** Not every innovation has to be a massive overhaul. Fixing small things can make a difference, too—often greater than you'd imagine. Look for the proverbial low-hanging fruit.

3. **Listen for people muttering, "There's got to be a better way."** For every annoying process, there is likely a simpler, more efficient, more elegant way to do it.

4. **Pay attention to happy accidents.** Remember penicillin? An intended use for one product or service may wind up being useful in other ways. Serendipity also plays an important role, so pay attention to chance meetings and unexpected encounters that can add value.

5. **Examine customer problems that aren't being solved.** Healthcare has a lot of these—and it has earned a reputation for overcomplicating procedures and policies that should be much simpler. Usually, the simplest solution is the best. Look for trends and issues that repeatedly crop up in patient satisfaction surveys (e.g., the food, the waste, the opaque billing) and aim to address big problems simply, creatively, and efficiently.

6. **Eliminate non-value-adding work.** What can we stop doing that isn't making a difference? And how can we spend the time gained on opportunities to solve problems creatively?

7. **Think big, but remember that problems of all sizes matter.** Have a vision—the innovator looks at things not as they are but as they could and should be. Don't be afraid to tackle an issue that seems mountain sized, yet don't ignore the one that's hill sized, either. All change matters, and improving one thing that everyone faces in a healthcare system shows thought, bravery, and fortitude.

We stand at the precipice of true change in our profession, a time when large healthcare organizations are examining ways to reduce waste; cut costs; and offer better, safer, higher-quality care with a leaner, better educated, more customer-centered staff. And whether we like it or not, change is coming hard and fast because, for far too long, healthcare organizations have complacently obfuscated and overcomplicated systems that shouldn't be so.

By assuming a fearless posture and inquisitive mind as you determine ways to innovate and change your organization, you'll be leading a profession that must figure out what it will ultimately become—and how it will get there. Change is the only static in healthcare; that is for certain.

EXERCISE 1

As you build your network, seek to meet creative, idea-generating people. Ask colleagues in other organizations what issues they've tackled and how.

EXERCISE 2

Make a list of problems and think of innovative ways to solve them by reading case studies, chatting with the colleagues you work with, and speaking to your peers in other organizations. What do you do well? What do you do well that could be expanded on? What could you do better?

RESOURCES

Clark, B., and S. Lindsey. 2013. "5 Ways Innovation Can Save Your Hospital." *Becker's Hospital Review*. Published September 16. www.beckershospitalreview.com/hospital-management -administration/5-ways-innovation-could-save-your-hospital .html.

Drucker, P. F. 1998. "The Discipline of Innovation." *Harvard Business Review* 76 (6): 149–57.

Herzlinger, R. E. 2014. "Innovating in Health Care—Framework." Harvard Business School Case No. 314-017. Boston: Harvard Business School Press.

Tucker, R. B. 2011. *Innovation Is Everybody's Business*. Hoboken, NJ: John Wiley & Sons.

White, K. R., R. Pillay, and X. Huang. 2016. "Nurse Leaders and the Innovation Competence Gap." *Nursing Outlook* 64 (3): 255–61.

Motivate Individuals and Teams

Innovative nurse leaders find a balance between their desire to get the work done and engaging others on their team to help shape that work. Amazing results can be achieved if we involve our team members early on and let them help form the final product. As Harry Truman said, "It is amazing what you can accomplish if you do not care who gets the credit."

—Kaye Bender, PhD, RN, FAAN, president and CEO, Public Health Accreditation Board, Alexandria, Virginia

SUCCESS ISN'T ALWAYS just hiring employees with the right qualifications; it often comes when motivation and engagement are channeled from the top. Strong leaders know how to pick talented, dedicated, and visionary employees and partners, of course—but they also encourage a can-do approach and cultivate momentum by gently urging and molding the wire frame of success into shape. In large organizations especially, success tends to be collective in spirit, not of the go-it-alone variety. So if "good people beget good people," as Dr. Thomas Frist Sr., one of HCA's founders, asserted, it's likely that people love to be empowered, to have ownership, and to be part of a winning team. And real leaders can cultivate just that.

Good leaders know how to motivate people to work toward common goals and to achieve positive, value-adding results. And organizations are always on the hunt for leaders who can inspire these traits in people. Any successful motivator must begin by leading with energy, conviction, and passion because the excitement rubs off on the team. The best leaders also inspire individuals to be willing to go that extra mile. If you're not able to motivate and engage your team to rally around the organization's goals, your results won't be of the highest possible quality.

The best leaders engage and empower people to recognize that the work they do is vital to the organization's mission, vision, and operation. They take an interest in individuals and help them feel vitally important, like a crucial part of the machinery that makes the place go. Employees, of course, want to know that their leader is united with them and appreciates how hard they're working. Once they understand a project and their role in it, if properly motivated and reinforced, they'll work hard to achieve the organization's mission. And the best leaders always offer their heartiest thanks and praise.

Although the following advice may seem commonsensical, many managers don't cultivate these habits—and they pay a price for it. As you advance in your career and develop your own style of managing and leading, remember these tips to nurture motivation and engagement among your troops:

- **Establish a clear vision.** Repeatedly articulating the organization's mission, vision, and values is a good way to ingrain them in individuals and teams. Understand what needs to be done and what the team's role is in doing it. Get input from your staff and others before making important decisions, and let your team have a say in what's decided and what will be achieved.
- **Choose the right projects.** "Management is doing things right; leadership is doing the right things," writes business guru Peter Drucker. This sentiment underscores the criticality of working on the right projects for the right reasons. Great leaders learn to focus at the levels that move their organization forward, knowing the difference between simple actions and actual results. If you

breathlessly spin through your workday without achieving goals that speak to your mission or vision, you're spreading yourself too thin and being ineffective. Don't take on too much at once; focus on only three to five goals at any given time. Doing so will lend focus to your team and will ensure that they do what they set out to do thoughtfully, thoroughly, and well.

- **Dissect and delegate.** Figure out what's to be done and who will be responsible for each component of the plan. Make assignments thoughtfully. Does the task fit the skills of the person who will be tackling it? Who are your most engaged workers? And does the person you're assigning to do the job have the authority, training, and tools needed to complete it?

- **Enable and fortify.** Give employees what they want and need. Don't just assume they have all the skills and tools they require to get the job done—check in with them personally and find out.

- **Ask, don't tell.** Everyone prefers to be asked to complete a job rather than be told what to do. Ask for opinions, best routes, and the like to enable and engage your colleagues and cultivate their ownership in the process. Allow them to teach you; let *them* tell *you* what they perceive is best. If you concur, let them determine major components of the action plan.

- **Say why it's important, and ask for input.** Paint a picture of the issue, sharing whatever details you have. "Our goal," you might say, "is to improve flow into and out of the operating room so that our patients won't be kept waiting as long. What ideas do you have? What can we do here?" Although you may know the desired outcome, your team may offer a variety of routes to get there that you hadn't previously considered. They'll also have a vested interest if they are empowered to come up with ideas to accomplish results.

- **Coach for success, and say thank you.** Feedback is a powerful motivator. Don't wait for their annual review to sing your staff's praises. Offer feedback—positive or gently negative—right away and as often as possible. Schedule regular meetings for updates and coaching. Show you're interested and available. And always say thank you, which is a huge reward in itself.
- **Be respectful, kind, fair, and trustworthy.** Create a supportive, healthy work environment. Respect confidences, and never get angry or send mixed messages. Don't embarrass employees in front of others. When problems arise, fully understand the context by examining all sides, and if the problem is yours to solve, make a decision. If you make a mistake, admit you were wrong and apologize. And never be afraid to laugh at yourself.
- **Care about people, not just their results.** Take time to get to know your employees, and always return their phone calls and e-mails. Be visible, check in for quick conversations to assess their workloads and stress levels, and offer help and resources if needed. Celebrate birthdays, and know in a general sense what issues they face at home. Recognize, too, that no one is at their best 100 percent of the time. An off day is just that, so be sure to look beyond it, especially when you've got a solidly talented crew.
- **Check in.** Take your employees' pulse from time to time, and understand how they feel about their progress toward a particular goal and any issues they're facing. Assess your team for diminishing engagement, flagging motivation, or exhaustion before it begins to crimp their progress and ultimate success. Ask them what needs changing and what's not going well; they'll tell you what needs to be done. Don't be afraid to take their suggestions and make midcourse corrections.

No one is an island. The ability to engage and motivate people is among the most critical facets of leadership. Cultivating these skills purposefully and thoughtfully through education and experience will sharpen your abilities as a fearless, intrepid, and inspiring leader. Treat others the way you want to be treated, work hard yourself, and expect great things of your phenomenal team—and success will surely come.

EXERCISE 1

Rate yourself on your ability to engage and motivate your team. Map out a recent project, noting what went right and what didn't. What could have been done better? Conduct a 360-degree review to understand the full perception of the project's effectiveness. Record these results in your journal.

EXERCISE 2

Volunteer for a project that offers you the opportunity to motivate and engage people.

RESOURCE

Nelson, B. 2012. *1501 Ways to Reward Employees*. New York: Workman Publishing Company.

SECTION III

Boost Your Career

AFTER I (DORRIE) spent my early career as a clinical nurse and clinical nurse specialist, I was invited to spend a semester teaching at the University of Maryland. A friend was on leave to study as a nurse practitioner and asked me to cover for her. I discovered I loved clinical teaching and spent the next 15 years teaching at Maryland in the undergraduate and graduate programs. Although I enjoyed preparing lectures for 300 students (we had large classes back then), my favorite part of teaching was taking eight students to clinical practicum, where each was responsible for up to three patients—so I needed to become familiar with 24 patients as well as all of the students' learning needs. The experience changed my career direction, and I returned to school part-time to earn my doctorate. Just think what might have happened had I not said yes to that opportunity!

Saying yes to opportunities is what makes you the master of your fate and puts you in charge of your career. During this time frame, I also wanted to become more active in my professional organization, the American Association of Critical-Care Nurses (AACN). I started out by attending meetings of my local chapter, volunteering for committees, and then becoming president of my local chapter. After being selected for national committees, I was elected to the AACN board of directors and eventually was chosen to be the association's president. Although these activities were all organizational service and not my day job, I learned as much about leadership from them as I did from my clinical and academic positions. I found incredible role models through AACN, including my favorite mentor, Kathy

Dracup, who was editor of *Heart & Lung: The Journal of Acute and Critical Care* (in which I published my very first paper) at the time and later of the *American Journal of Critical Care.*

Kathy saw me in a very long bathroom line at the National Teaching Institute (AACN's yearly educational conference), and, having recently been appointed dean at the University of California, San Francisco (UCSF), she encouraged me to apply for an opening there. I was happy on the East Coast and also had a ten-year-old. Kathy's response? "Perfect time to move!" Of course she meant: Move before your son starts high school. Although I was not looking for a new job, I went home and discussed the idea with my family. The opportunity grew on me, and a year later we moved 2,800 miles across the country and I became the academic associate dean at UCSF. What a joy! And what if I had been too afraid to leave the East Coast?

Ken has learned much over the course of his career, too. He once accepted a position as vice president of operations only to learn that either he or a colleague of the same rank would be named chief operating officer. The near-impossible competition and ill feelings that ensued were good neither for the organization nor for the people involved. Within two years, Ken and his colleague had both moved on, still harboring uncomfortable feelings. A decade later, they reconnected in a different capacity. Healthcare management, Ken learned, is a small community—so never burn bridges.

Like me, Ken also learned to embrace serendipity. He came to healthcare leadership as a result of a series of school closings, forced transfers, and hallway conversations. Choosing nursing, then pivoting toward healthcare management, then returning to nursing allowed him to sample each trajectory—and each, in turn, informed the way he worked with and understood clinicians, academics, and administrators. And he's never looked back.

One final story: I recall a former star student of ours who, after completing his master's degree, rapidly moved through the early phases of his career to become a nurse manager. But the job made him miserable, and he ultimately realized he wasn't using his gifts.

He'd always wanted to work with children and eventually became an elementary schoolteacher. Today, he is a happy, well-adjusted elementary school principal. Sometimes we have to spend a lot of time, energy, and resources following one direction to find the correct path. We just need to be open to opportunities and not feel there are points in life where it's just "too late in the game."

Now that you've learned what it takes to manage yourself and your job—and perhaps have a few successes under your belt—you can begin to think about how to position yourself to take charge of your career.

Note that we have transitioned our language from the concept of "manage" in the titles of the first two sections to giving your nursing leadership career a "boost" in this section. The idea is that you really can't advance your career without first mastering yourself and your job. Once you've tackled the lessons in sections I and II, where will you make your career take *you*?

—Dorrie Fontaine

Orchestrate Your Career

Nurses are generally benevolent people. We worry about others and go out of our way to be helpful no matter the personal sacrifice. Unfortunately, that concern is not always reciprocated. No one is going to look out for your welfare better than you can yourself, so make your career decisions based on what is best for you. Weigh the pros and cons and ask others for advice, of course, but listen above all to your inner voice and be sure the choices are good for you. It's okay to be a little selfish when your future is at stake.

—Pamela F. Cipriano, PhD, RN, NEA-BC, FAAN, president (2014–2018), American Nurses Association

You alone are responsible for taking charge of your career. Your spouse, mentor, sponsor, coach, or boss may have an interest in your success, but it's solely up to you to determine the particulars of your trajectory. *You* are the only one who can make your professional dreams come true.

So develop a solid and honest understanding of yourself. Identify your gifts and your passions, and then set a course and create career goals. Write out a professional development plan (see lesson 41) for achieving those goals. Remember that this plan is a fluid document and that all such plans must be flexible and open to serendipity. Remember, too, that some of the jobs you will hold over the course of your career probably have not even been invented yet.

Focus your energy on solving problems and adding value to the organization where you work. Don't waste energy blaming the environment, the economy, or others for what's wrong. Difficult issues and people will always exist, and your job is to solve the problems that are in your scope and to let go of others that are beyond your professional control. You will find that with intensity of purpose and focus, you can accomplish a great deal.

Here are some ideas to help you become the captain of your career ship:

- **Have a clear idea of what you want to do and what you're good at.** Do you want to be a hospital CNO, COO, or CEO, or would you prefer to manage the hospital's care coordination functions? Are you interested in serving vulnerable populations? Are you attracted to academic medical centers, or do for-profit institutions excite you more? Consider geography, your desired salary, and the size of institution you'd like to work in as well as your family's needs on the home front. Don't pursue opportunities or ideas that are clearly pipe dreams or so unrealistic that they're untenable. Dream—but be grounded, too.
- **Write and maintain a professional development plan.** Review and update your plan at least every year.
- **Be exceptional in your current job.** The best way toward a new, better job is to do your very best work in your current one. Employers seek executives with a proven track record of meaningful accomplishments. Be a problem solver—look for problems in your current gig and solve them thoughtfully and competently.
- **Focus on personal growth.** Learn new skills, expand your strengths, and stretch your limits. Your professional development plan will help you identify what to work on. Seek assignments that will challenge you.

- **Look beyond the confines of your job.** Young professionals often find themselves in positions with a narrow focus. Broaden your horizon by volunteering for projects that expose you to larger issues in your organization. For example, you might volunteer to assess a community need and develop recommendations—and ultimately programs—to address that need. Along the way, you will meet people whom you can add to your professional network.
- **Seek out effective mentors.** "Ms. Smith," you might say, "I admire the way you work with the medical staff. Would you share with me some of the tactics you use?" Understand that as a protégé, *you* are responsible for doing the most work. Some early careerists mistakenly think that they can just sit back and wait for their mentor to call them with advice. In point of fact, the one being mentored is the one who must actively pursue opportunities through the mentor, never forgetting to be unfailingly polite and grateful. Ask your mentor questions such as the following:
  - What's the logical next step up on the career ladder from my current job?
  - Do I have the education and experience required for that next step? If not, what degree, certification, or experience do I need to qualify?
  - Whom should I meet to begin the path toward my ideal job?

As you consider what's next, accept that if you're no longer learning and growing in your current position—even if you're still contributing—it may be time to move on. It's *your* career and *your* life, and *you* should be the one who decides when and where to move on. Be the best captain you can be.

EXERCISE 1

Join the American Nurses Association or another professional nursing association and get involved. Aim to meet people in different positions of leadership and keep apprised of the job opportunities that are currently available. Discuss these opportunities with close colleagues and others in your network to get a sense of the positions' requirements (e.g., education, certifications, type and duration of previous work experience).

EXERCISE 2

Undergo a 360-degree evaluation to identify what you're good at and the areas in which you can improve.

RESOURCES

Dye, C. F., and A. N. Garman. 2015. *Exceptional Leadership: 16 Critical Competencies for Healthcare Executives*, 2nd ed. Chicago: Health Administration Press.

Goldsmith, M., with M. Reiter. 2007. *What Got You Here Won't Get You There: How Successful People Become Even More Successful*. New York: Hyperion.

McBride, A. B. 2011. *The Growth and Development of Nurse Leaders*. New York: Springer.

Palmer, P. J. 2000. *Let Your Life Speak: Listening for the Voice of Vocation*. San Francisco: Jossey-Bass.

Lead Positive Change

Positive change must always begin by painting a bold vision for the future that keeps the patient at its center. That vision must be created in a way that inspires ownership and moves the hearts of nurses to become leaders in the journey. Never underestimate the power of a carefully crafted vision to enable positive change.

—Amelia S. Black, DNP, RN, NEA-BC, chief operating officer, Sentara Martha Jefferson Hospital, Charlottesville, Virginia

CHANGE IS THE only constant in life, according to a millennia-old adage, and this certainly holds true for healthcare today. The ability to manage and lead change in an organization is a major expectation for success as a nurse leader.

The *transformational* leader articulates a vision of the future that can be shared with peers, team members, and other stakeholders while paying high attention to their different values, ideals, morals, and needs. The transformational leader uses the mission, vision, and values of an organization to guide decisions that "transform" or move it down a new path with different expectations, structures, systems, and outcomes, even as the conditions keep changing. This leadership approach is far different from the historical *transactional* one, in which the leader meted out rewards and punishments to motivate and elicit the desired behaviors from subordinates.

To lead positive change, consider the following:

- **Cultivate a high degree of emotional intelligence.** Emotional intelligence is the capacity to be aware of and control your emotions and to manage interpersonal relationships with others empathetically. How have you continued to hone your emotional intelligence?
- **Have a high degree of social savvy.** How keen an interest do you show in others? Do you nurture relationships and build effective networks and coalitions? (See lessons 6 and 43.)
- **Engage in visioning.** What vision do you share with your peers, team members, and other stakeholders that is consistent with your organization's vision? Think big!
- **Align values with goals.** Nothing is more effective than telling specific stories about how values are enacted. What the organization values should be showcased, so catch people in the act and tell their story!
- **Develop a strategic mind-set, and cultivate it in others.** When a course correction is needed, it is important to set goals and, even more important, to engage in scenario planning. Be willing to try something new (see lesson 35).
- **Make decisions that align with organizational strategies and goals.** When you know your goals are in alignment with your organization's, zero in on the areas that will have the biggest impact. Seek to be the best in something—choose excellence!
- **Seek out champions and partnerships.** Find like-minded people and organizations in your community, network, or profession to help you attain your goals. If one organizational goal is to develop or expand palliative care services, find champions in your ranks and also look outside the organization for community agencies (e.g., hospices, home health services, volunteer groups, foundations) that can join forces with you to build momentum.

- **Collaborate interprofessionally.** In healthcare, the chances of success are greater if you approach problem solving and decision making with input from colleagues in diverse professions.
- **Use wisdom to manage the unknowable.** The authors of *On The Edge: Nursing in an Age of Complexity* contend that in a chaotic, complex environment such as healthcare, nurse leaders must be able to mobilize the right people, encourage sensemaking, change direction on a dime, and be nimble at trying different things. You can beat your head against the wall and use a lot of resources without solving the problem. Or, by accepting the nonlinear perspective of complexity science, you can do something relatively simple that yields a huge benefit in terms of outcome and reach—and manage the unknowable!

EXERCISE 1

Think about decisions you have made. Which decisions resulted in the highest yield in terms of organizational alignment (as evidenced by the response you received from senior leaders, organizational attention to your efforts, and the way they were rewarded)? What factors contributed to the success (or failure) of your decisions? For example, what role did timing play? Who was involved in gathering information and reaching the decision? What was the level of corporate readiness?

EXERCISE 2

Recall a situation that generated polarizing discussions, many of which hinged on negative energy. How would you respond to conversations and points of view that do not invoke positive energy and optimism? Practice what you would say to a group or to individuals who seem to focus only on the negatives.

RESOURCES

Dye, D. F., and A. N. Garman. 2014. *Exceptional Leadership: 16 Critical Competencies for Healthcare Executives*, 2nd ed. Chicago: Health Administration Press.

Lindberg, C., S. Nash, and C. Lindberg. 2008. *On The Edge: Nursing in an Age of Complexity.* Bordentown, NJ: Plexus Press.

Maxfield, D. 2013. "5 Steps for Leaders Struggling to Lead Positive Change." Published July 11. http://chiefexecutive.net /5-steps-for-leaders-struggling-to-lead-positive-change/.

Plews-Ogan, M., and G. Beyt. 2014. *Wisdom Leadership in Academic Health Science Centers: Leading Positive Change.* London: Radcliffe Publishing.

Know and Use Your Strengths

Knowing your strengths doesn't always mean being strong. As you work with your colleagues and subordinates, you will sometimes be called on to be empathetic and human in the midst of making strategic decisions. Being human as a leader is a valuable skill but requires development and practice. This skill is portable and can be taken with you as you pursue new and different opportunities.

—Ginger Cohen, MS, RN, FACHE, clinical sales liaison, Coram CVS / Specialty Infusion Services, Fort Worth, Texas

WHAT *REALLY* GETS you out of bed and amped up to work in the morning? What parts of your job do you sing (rather than slog) your way through? What professional domains ignite your passion?

Learning your strengths and using them effectively is a key to success in any field, healthcare included. Strengths may be things that you're good at or that you enjoy, but ideally they're both. They can be overarching qualities ("I like taking the helm of a project") or specific and task oriented ("I like creating spreadsheets"), but they should be *yours*. Identifying what you're good at and how you like to spend your time comes first.

There was a time when people thought that working on weaknesses was the best way to become a well-rounded professional. But the reverse is really true. Knowing your strengths will be an advantage throughout your career.

Once you identify what you're good at, do those things as often as you can. Surround yourself with people whose own strengths complement yours, not people who are carbon copies of you and your assets. If you're a great leader but are weak in finance, for example, aim for a leadership position and recruit talented professionals who can support and oversee the organization's finances. If you're better at behind-the-scenes activities and prefer to keep your nose to the grindstone working on tasks rather than on big, messy, visionary projects with few parameters, acknowledge this about yourself. There is no shame in or advantage to either. So own the skin you're in—you'll be happier in the long run being yourself.

That said, don't expect your job to relentlessly please you once you've identified your favorite tasks—no job offers constant fun. Just know how to relish the time you do spend doing things you love.

So how do you figure out what you're good at? Here are a few questions to get you started:

- What do you get excited about doing?
- When you've been successful, what specific strengths did you tap?
- What do others say you're good at?
- What's been revealed to you in your performance reviews?
- How do your customers, patients, or clients view you?
- Do you see a difference between what you like doing and what you're good at? Or are they the same?

Some professionals keep a journal, listing projects they've worked on and what enabled their success. Rating each project on a ten-point scale may reveal what personal gifts you used en route. Others undergo formal analyses (e.g., the Myers-Briggs assessment, the VIA Survey) to identify their tendencies and assets. Still others tap professional coaches, who can help identify strengths and address weaknesses.

Following are a few more suggestions:

- **Beware of thinking you will always be weak in an area because of early negative experiences.** People change and grow, honing and developing skills over the course of their lives. Just because you were a rotten math student (or think you were) doesn't mean you will always be bad at finance. Some deficits can be addressed with education and practice, and as a result, some qualities you consider weaknesses may actually become strengths. Don't simply assume that your weaknesses are cast in cement because of your past.
- **Don't get lazy with your strengths.** Just like regular exercise, your strengths need to be used regularly to ensure their fitness. Don't assume you'll always be good at something if you never practice it or never seek out tasks to stretch and further cultivate what you're good at. Keep those asset muscles toned.
- **Develop an elevator speech.** Learn to describe your greatest strengths in two or three sentences so that you'll be prepared to introduce yourself and convey your skills to influential people quickly and competently without braggadocio. Assert your assets and own them comfortably. If the CEO of your company got on the elevator with you, and you had two floors to tell her about yourself, what would you say? *Know this in advance.*

You can follow these tips merely by taking the time to know yourself. Once you've done that, you'll use your strengths to your advantage—just by knowing what they are.

EXERCISE 1

Keep a journal, listing projects you've worked on. Note the strengths you used and the outcome of each project. As you review your journal, look for patterns. What role did you play in your most successful projects? Were you the leader, or did you serve in another capacity? Studying your own track record will give you a good indication of where your true strengths lie.

EXERCISE 2

Prepare an elevator speech describing your greatest strengths in two to three sentences. Then practice your elevator speech with your mentor or friends. Practice makes perfect!

RESOURCES

Buckingham, M., and D. O. Clifton. 2001. *Now, Discover Your Strengths.* New York: The Free Press.

Rath, T. 2007. *StrengthsFinder 2.0.* New York: Gallup Press.

Choose Your Mentor

The importance of finding good mentors cannot be overstated. Mentors are strategic risk takers and good communicators, and they provide key support and guidance at critical junctures in one's professional trajectory. Drawing on their own leadership experience, they help clarify goals, establish priorities, identify knowledge or skill gaps, and offer encouragement through the difficult patches that everyone experiences. Most successful leaders have been helped by a number of mentors at various points in their career, sometimes only briefly and sometimes over the course of an entire career.

—Kathleen Dracup, RN, FNP, PhD, FAAN, dean emerita and professor emerita, University of California San Francisco School of Nursing, San Francisco

EACH OF US is the product of a variety of influences. Consider the people you've crossed paths with during your life who have exerted an influence on you: Your family, teachers, coworkers, and friends have all made their mark on your personality, perspective, aspirations, and work ethic. The lessons you take away from others and the way you synthesize and internalize what others say and do (either by mimicking it or by moving far away from it) shape who you ultimately become, how effectively you work, and, in many ways, how successful your career is.

But unlike your family, teachers, and coworkers—who were essentially assigned to you—your professional mentors are actively chosen by you and for a number of reasons. You choose professional mentors from your workplace, school, or professional associations to impart advice, share knowledge, and serve as sounding boards. They can help you widen your network, improve your resume, and coach you as you prepare for an interview. The best mentors always take your calls and give you honest opinions. Mentors don't have to be in the same field as you or even in a job that you consider to be your dream gig. Most important is that they possess traits you admire and want and that you feel comfortable with them.

In the mentor–protégé relationship, the formality of the arrangement is up to you. It can be casual; you do not need to declare someone as your mentor so much as to connect with him or her on a regular basis, communicating about issues that concern you, deficits you perceive in yourself, and problems you're having at work. They will likely be flattered that you consider them a guide, even if the arrangement is informal.

Others may feel more comfortable establishing a regular meeting schedule with their mentors, defining expectations, and charting a path of focus. Some mentors and mentees even document the terms of their relationship in writing to keep themselves organized and honest. The parameters of schedule and relationship are entirely up to you and your mentor.

The key is to snag the opportunity when it presents itself—and sometimes that happens unexpectedly. If you meet someone you like who shows an interest in your career, you might ask, "Would you be willing to mentor me for the next few months while I try to improve my leadership skills?" or "Will you help me with my job search? I seem to be having problems during interviews." Most mentors are glad to pay it forward for the help they received over the course of their own careers, and they feel organically happy to help an ambitious young professional who is eager to learn. Being a good student is the best way to show gratitude to your mentor, and so is serving as a mentor yourself when the opportunity presents itself down the line.

How do you identify good mentors? Look for individuals who exhibit a caring nature, a commitment to others, a generosity of spirit, and a willingness to be readily available and to take risks. It really is okay—and it's sometimes even necessary—to have multiple and different mentors on your journey in nursing.

So where do you find these mentors?

- Former professors or supervisors, especially if they're recently retired, likely have time to help.
- Peers often make excellent mentors, especially if they have facility that you lack in a certain domain.
- Professionals whose fields touch yours tangentially can offer a valuable perspective or a way of thinking that you otherwise might not have considered.
- Senior executives, including university deans and tenured professors, often make great mentors because they have a lot of experience as well as an inclination to help.
- Colleagues who have three to five years' more experience than you are ideal because they have just traveled the path that you hope to take.

Occasionally, more formal routes to choosing a mentor are available. Some universities, professional associations, and companies have mentoring programs that pair seasoned executives with new ones. But not everyone has a pool of appropriate mentors from which to choose, and if you've determined that you need a mentor, it may be up to you to find one.

If you sense a scarcity of qualified casual mentors around you, consider investing money in hiring a career coach. Coaches—paid professionals, often certified—are another route to developing your best self and making good decisions. These "mentors for pay" can be useful in all the ways more casual mentors can be, but they also often bring expertise in a certain field, such as healthcare, and may prove to be an excellent investment during a difficult job search or transition. You also have the benefit of reliable accessibility, given that it's a service you're paying for.

Whatever the arrangement, understand that *you* are responsible for the bulk of the work. You're tapping a source, whether you're paying for it or not and whether it's a formal arrangement or casual, so be ready to take on the more active role in the relationship. Arrange regular meetings with your mentor, and stay in touch by phone and e-mail. When you need help, ask for it—but always be respectful of your mentor's time.

You will need mentors throughout your career, so nurture and maintain these relationships even after the bulk of the mentoring has transpired. Don't dump people after they've helped you; remember them, respect them, and recall the messages they gave you. Send them periodic notes long after regular contact has subsided. Remind them that they served a critical function in your career and that you owe them your gratitude—and much else besides. Your thoughtfulness will, most likely, be more than enough thanks for them.

EXERCISE 1

Make a list of people who have mentored you during your personal and professional life, and list the issues they've helped you deal with. Also consider the colleagues who have provided you with advice and perspectives about specific issues.

EXERCISE 2

Draft a written statement about what you hope to gain from your mentor. Prepare a formal agreement, and use it with your mentor.

RESOURCES

Dye, C. F., and A. N. Garman. 2015. "Mentors: Finding and Engaging for Maximum Input." In *Exceptional Leadership: 16 Critical Competencies for Healthcare Executives*, 2nd ed., 205–11. Chicago: Health Administration Press.

International Coach Federation. 2016. "Coaching with Distinction." http://coachfederation.org.

Jenkins, C. Y., J. S. Lindsey, and J. Andrews. 2014. "Mentoring: A Tool for Building Your Career." www.box.net/shared/e4 bxa219ad.

McBride, A. B. 2011. *The Growth and Development of Nurse Leaders*. New York: Springer.

Plews-Ogan, M., and G. Beyt. 2014. *Wisdom Leadership in Academic Health Science Centers: Leading Positive Change*. London: Radcliffe Publishing.

Create a Professional
Development Plan

An important step in developing a professional development plan is being self-aware and discovering your leadership style and strengths. Be open to feedback and ongoing mentoring and development. Volunteer for stretch assignments and projects that will help you learn what kind of work you enjoy. Become involved in professional organizations and network to expand your way of thinking. Spend time reflecting on your goals because new roles may be created that do not exist today. Ongoing education will open more doors and possibilities. The great thing about a professional development plan is that you can change it as you gain knowledge and insights about what you really want to do.

—Joyce A. Batcheller, DNP, RN, NEA-BC, FAAN, nurse executive advisor, AMN Healthcare, San Diego, California, and adjunct faculty, Texas Tech University Health Sciences Center School of Nursing, Lubbock, Texas

IT'S EASY, ESPECIALLY early in your career, to cast about aimlessly and let the world happen *to* you. Many young careerists, unsure of their direction, end up wasting valuable time and effort this way. But absence of a decision is still a decision. With a bit of focus and planning at the outset and all through your professional life, you can reap the rewards down the line. And the best place to begin that focus is with a professional development plan (PDP).

Developing a PDP or career plan—essentially a map of your desired professional trajectory—is one of the best ways you can harness direction. The plan itself doesn't have to be long, fancy, or formally written or contain more than a few pages of notes that mean something to you. The important thing is to take the time to consider your strengths and hopes, jot them down, and then revisit them every year or so as you move into your chosen profession, pivot between jobs, undertake key assignments, or identify new interests or directions. You might be surprised how dramatically your situation can change in just a few short years.

Ken recalls conducting a mock interview with a new master's student who repeatedly twirled and dropped his pencil. The student's PDP asserted that he wanted to be a hospital chief nursing officer within a decade—a plan that, at the time, seemed hard to imagine. Today, however, seven years after graduate school and three promotions, he not only is a successful hospital nursing director but also says he owes his success to having a plan he stuck to.

A PDP will help you identify your skills and passions. Knowing these will, in turn, enable you to decide what sort of job is a strong match for your skills. And although no absolutely perfect job exists, having a plan will steer you toward the best possible opportunities. The earlier in your career you identify what you want out of your professional life, the better.

PDPs aren't only useful on paper. If you're able to verbalize the things that really excite you, your mentor, friends, and colleagues might be able to offer perspective about what they see in you and suggest ideas, job prospects, and companies that are a prudent match for you. Hearing what others say and perceive about you can be just as valuable as knowing what enlivens your mind and sustains your interest. So take the time to talk about your professional goals with others and listen to what they say. The best mentors will hear you, process the information, and offer you perspective about your best trajectory and possible next steps.

Begin crafting your PDP by jotting down the answers to these questions:

- **What gifts and skills do I possess?** These talents can be difficult to ferret out on your own, so ask your parents, mentors, friends, supervisors, and colleagues to help you identify them. Those who have just taken on a leadership role might undergo a personality test, such as the Myers-Briggs assessment, to reveal their strengths, traits, and predilections. Some nurse administrators find it helpful to keep a personal project journal that details the challenges they've tackled with poise and precision. If you've got a job or two under your belt, consider jotting down some notes about a few projects that have meant something to you, what you liked about them, and why they succeeded. A task that allowed you to sample a certain area of work that you ended up enjoying is sometimes enough to reroute an entire career path.
- **Where are my deficits?** Are you too fussy, or are you not detail oriented enough? Are you disorganized? Are you overly sensitive? What skills do you need to hone? Create a personal to-do list.
- **What am I passionate about?** Just knowing what you're good at isn't enough; determine what really excites and engages you. Are there volunteer positions that have captured your imagination? People with whom you'd be thrilled to work? Certain types of initiatives that deeply interest you? In your ideal world, are you a teacher, an explorer, a researcher, an organizer, a storyteller—or all of the above?
- **How did I get where I am?** Review your work history, the timeline of what you've done over your career. What were your significant turning points? Who played significant roles?
- **What's my ideal job?** Make a list of positions you might want to pursue. Do these jobs require additional training and education? More years of experience? Is any particular job feasible at the moment, or is it a long-term goal?

- **Where do I want to live?** Have you considered living abroad? Are there states or regions of the country you love, or places you'd *never* want to live? Or are you determined to keep to a particular zip code, sticking close to family and friends? Understand your practical professional parameters, and remember that while limiting your geographic area is okay, you may also be limiting your opportunities.
- **What are my target companies?** There are dream jobs, so there are dream organizations, too. As part of your PDP, list between 10 and 20 organizations you admire in which you would want to work. Learn more about each prospective employer. Read up on the people who populate the organization, including their backgrounds, experience, and education levels. Ask others what they've heard about the place. Get a sense of its flavor, its mission and vision, and its history. As you gather facts, the company may come off your list—or move up to the top.

Put as much effort as you can into your PDP, but remember that it's not a showpiece like a resume or a curriculum vitae. It's a practical document that's as fluid, alive, and dynamic as you are. Let *it* focus *you*. Having a PDP road map will help you achieve a career at the intersection of your gifts and your passions.

EXERCISE 1

Create a PDP using the questions above.

EXERCISE 2

Ask a couple of trusted colleagues to describe what they think you are best at doing, especially in a leadership role. Then ask them to tell you where you could use some coaching. At the same time, write down what *you* perceive your strengths and deficits to be. Did your perceived strengths and weaknesses match those that your colleagues identified? Pay attention to discrepancies as areas for further focus.

RESOURCES

Dye, C. F., and A. N. Garman. 2015. "Sample Self-Development Plan." In *Exceptional Leadership: 16 Critical Competencies for Healthcare Executives*, 2nd ed., 257–58. Chicago: Health Administration Press.

Scivicque, C. 2011. "Creating Your Professional Development Plan: 3 Surprising Truths." *Forbes*. Posted June 21. www.forbes.com/sites/work-in-progress/2011/06/21/creating-your-professional-development-plan-3-surprising-truths/.

Build Your Resume

People often make complex decisions in the blink of an eye and based on very little information. In hiring, an applicant's resume makes the first impression of that individual's qualifications for a particular opportunity. Use your resume to chronologize your professional accomplishments, to measure the outcomes of your work, and to portray your values and choices. Spend time to ensure the document that will be securing you an interview and representing your career is well thought out, truthful, and free of arbitrary and subjective superlatives.

—Heather Kopecky, PhD, MBA, RN, senior client partner, Korn Ferry International, Los Angeles, California

A RESUME'S SOLE purpose—the *only* reason for its existence—is to get you an interview with a prospective employer. Given the weight of its single, critical role, you'd be wise to put some degree of thought, effort, and creativity into it. Your resume should succinctly tell your story *and* clearly demonstrate how you can help employers solve the problems they're experiencing. Both of those components are equally important.

But before all that, consider what you need to do to get the kind of job you want. As you acquire the education, skills, and experience needed to achieve your professional goals, add them to your resume. By mapping out that plan on paper, in your mind, and verbally with others, you'll find you've got a lot of bragging points.

Here are a few tips for creating or updating your resume:

- **Consider its style.** As with dress, writing, and oral presentation, style matters. The historical resume—a format that presents a timeline tally of your education, professional experience, accomplishments, skills, and awards in chronological order, most recent first—is the resume style most commonly used in healthcare and the type most employers are looking for. If you've got a curriculum vitae–style resume, consider reformatting it if you're interviewing for a management position. Otherwise it may seem dissonant and opaque to your interviewers. Ultimately, it may also mean that the interview door remains tightly shut. So keep your resume accessible.

- **Quantify your work and results.** Populate your resume with work that achieved measurable results. If you haven't done work that is quantifiable in some way, volunteer for such projects. This experience will reap dividends when it comes time to update your resume. Have you helped reduce a hospital's infection rate? Led initiatives in diabetes education and nutrition counseling in the community? Improved customer service? Supervised a large staff, helped populate certain staffing areas, or overseen national research grants as part of your job? If so, quantify what you've done. Consider the power of saying, for example, that you've "led a project that reduced hospital infection rates by 5 percent over two years." Figure out how to capture your work in this way—and capitalize on it.

- **Use action words.** You didn't just have a staff of 30; you *led* a staff of 30 direct reports. You weren't just responsible for sales, imaging, and nurse hires; you "increased sales by 15 percent over the previous year," "spurred an 8 percent growth in imaging volume between 2016 and 2017," and "recruited two dozen nurses to populate eight units, bringing each unit up by 25 percent to proper staffing levels."

Consider these points, too:

- You need only one resume, so don't spend a huge amount of time crafting different resumes for different positions that highlight and showcase different talents. The majority of your time is best spent networking.
- You don't need to state a career objective in your resume—you can do so in a cover letter or during an interview. Remember that the purpose of the resume is to provide a profile or snapshot of your experience and skills. More critical is how you leverage your network so that your resume gets funneled to the right person and lands you that interview.
- Always keep your resume to one or two pages, adding more pages only after you gain considerable experience. More important than its length is covering the most important points concisely.
- Include all of your jobs in chronological order, starting with the most recent. Jobs you held more than ten years ago and temporary work may be listed without detail. If you worked several jobs during college, you can group them together.
- List the dates (month and year) of your graduation and any honors. Your degrees should be listed *exactly* as they appear on your diploma. For example, if you earned a master of science degree in nursing administration but your diploma says only "master of science," that is what you put on your resume.
- Provide three to five bullet points for each work entry. Emphasize your most recent experience by including more detail. Your prospective employer will look most closely at and be most interested in what's happened lately. For each entry, balance job responsibilities with quantifiable accomplishments. Ask yourself "How did I add value?" and "What will I be remembered for?" Your work entries should not read like a job description.
- *Never* attach a picture to your resume.

- *Never* overstate your role or accomplishments. If you were a summer intern during graduate school and helped design a nurse residency program, do not say that you developed a nurse residency program. Instead, describe what your contribution was.
- Make sure your resume has absolutely perfect spelling and grammar. Even if it makes you feel awkward, have someone whom you trust proofread your resume for errors. Errors = no interview. Don't embarrass yourself—be sure it's right.

Everyone has a unique opinion about resumes, interviews, and cover letters—but know that no matter what, the classic approach is best. Beware of asking too many people for advice or heeding oddball recommendations to get noticed in an ocean of applicants. In the end, who and what you are—and where you come from—will be your best selling points. Your resume gets the door open a crack; the rest is all you.

EXERCISE 1

Pull out the resume that you completed in college or for your last job interview, and update it.

EXERCISE 2

Ask someone to critique your resume and to suggest ways to improve it.

RESOURCE

Tyler, J. L. 2011. *Tyler's Guide: The Healthcare Executive's Job Search*, 4th ed. Chicago: Health Administration Press.

LESSON 43

Grow Your Network

Two decades ago, when we began our controversial research on family presence during resuscitation, there were no networks. As we published our findings from multiple studies, we deliberately built a network of like-minded people. We partnered nationally with nurses, physicians, social workers, respiratory therapists, chaplains, and family members. We expanded our network to include hospital administrators, lawyers, ethicists, publishers, professional organizations, and members of the media. Networks can be a catalyst for changing healthcare and making a difference in the lives of our patients and their families.

—Cathie E. Guzzetta, PhD, RN, FAAN, clinical professor, George Washington University School of Nursing, Washington, DC

THE TERM *NETWORKING* is used a lot in the working world for good reason: Everyone grasps its importance. What's less clear is exactly how to build a network, how to expand it, and how to maintain it. Many mistakenly assume that people with strong networks are simply lucky, popular, and easygoing; that they find socializing a breeze; and that they can work a room with poise and ease.

For most of us, networking is indeed hard work. But as a tool to find your next job, advance your career, and meet other like-minded people, nothing is more important—and often, nothing is more satisfying.

It's impossible to underestimate the criticality of networking. Roughly eight in ten people land nursing leadership and other healthcare jobs through effective networking. And as you progress up the career ladder, you'll have (and require) a growing network of professional relationships on which to rely.

So what is networking? Simply put, it's establishing mutually beneficial professional relationships. And often, the most effective way to begin a networking relationship is to offer yourself in service to others. Can you tell someone about a job opening? Can you provide a reference? Do you have a unique perspective or experience with a hospital, school, or company? Can you link two people together who have similar career trajectories?

If you're helpful to others first, your relationships will have a high chance of success and longevity because people remember those who have helped them professionally. And down the line, you may be on the receiving end of the relationship—getting important job advice, obtaining a reference, hearing about an open position, or being invited to meet with a mutual colleague. There really are only "six degrees of separation," and networking makes the world feel smaller and more manageable.

Networking has four basic components: building, organizing, growing, and maintaining your network.

1.   **Build it.** Each of us already has some kind of a network, even if many of us don't recognize it as such—so you won't be starting completely from scratch. Think of your family, friends, neighbors, classmates, teachers, clergy, and business associates. Consider fellow members of clubs, alumni groups, trade associations, and church congregations. Recall former coworkers and employees, and even those of your spouse or partner. Tap your children's friends' parents or those you know through the local schools.

Then consider those outside your existing circles. Do you know anyone who might know successful people you would like to meet in your target specialty? Might casual links through friends, family, and coworkers enable you to set up a meeting or informational interview with someone at a company you admire? You might tell your neighbor you're hoping to launch a career in a nursing specialty. "Do you know anyone," you could ask, "who could help me learn about the field?" Let that be your refrain.

2. **Organize it.** Use LinkedIn and other social media as a way to connect with those you know, those you'd like to know, hospitals or companies that interest you, and others in your field. Read trade publications to learn about job transitions and promotions. Keep your contact list and network database organized and up to date; when you hear of a change, record it immediately. Keeping this information updated and accurate is critical.

3. **Grow it.** People often focus on expanding their networks when they're hunting for a job but then stop reaching out once they've landed one. That's a mistake. Think of networking like regular exercise—pay attention to it throughout your career. Connect online with those you've just met, and then stay connected via e-mail (sending interesting articles or congratulations on job anniversaries or new consulting gigs) and occasionally in person. Routinely tap people in your network with the question, "Who else should I be meeting?"

   Also remember the value of volunteering (see lesson 27). Participation in nursing organizations is a great way to fortify your network and meet like-minded individuals. Offer to speak at an upcoming meeting or to write articles for a newsletter. As you grow your network, however, remember to be both discreet and sensitive to your current employer. Use sound judgment when networking or meeting with competitors in your market.

4. **Maintain it.** You can maintain your network by sending pertinent and interesting articles by e-mail and LinkedIn

postings (but do this judiciously, taking care not to become one of those who constantly forward e-mails). Or, you can write quick but thoughtful notes, make phone calls, and occasionally meet in person. Remember which topics those in your network find meaningful: "Ms. Jones," you might write, "I'm sending you this article because I remember you said you were interested in developing a diabetes program at your hospital. I hope you find it useful. Do let me know if I can ever be of assistance."

Staying connected with those in your network doesn't have to be a time-consuming burden. Suggest meeting your contacts for morning coffee before work, a quick lunch, or a brief hello at a local industry event. Set a goal of meeting someone in your network at least once a month. Be sure to include contacts from companies other than your current employer. Talk shop and ask questions. Discuss problems you're facing and solicit opinions.

EXERCISE 1

The next time you attend a reception or function, look at the list of attendees and identify people you'd like to meet. Learn as much as you can about the organizations represented by attendees and the reasons people are attending the event. Arrive early, and do your best to meet the people who you think can help you. As you meet people, give them your contact information, ask for theirs, and send them a quick note soon after the event.

EXERCISE 2

Update the contact information of the people in your network. Make a list of people you would like to add to your network.

RESOURCES

American Nurses Association. 2015. "Professional Networking for Nurses." Published April. http://nursingworld.org /Professional-Networking-for-Nurses.

Casciaro, T., F. Gino, and M. Kouchaki. 2016. "Learn to Love Networking." *Harvard Business Review* 94 (5): 104–7.

Interview Well

A thoughtful, well-organized resume may secure you an invitation to interview, but a strong and compelling interview will help you win the prize. Take this in-person opportunity seriously, yet have fun with it and learn from it because one day you may be on the other side of the interview table.

—Kathryn Sugerman, RN, MSN, MBA, partner, Spencer Stuart, New York

LIKE MANY THINGS in life, a successful job interview begins with good preparation. You should prepare for an interview as you would prepare for a big game or an important test: with focus, organization, and precision. Consider your qualifications, your passions, and your personal stories. Imagine several lines of questioning and the answers you'd provide. Figure out why and how you're a solid match for the company you may be working for.

Here are some tips to help you prepare for an interview:

- **Know what you're getting into.** Be sure you know what format the interview will take: Is it with a single person or a group? How formal is it? Try to find out how long the meeting will last, and put aside at least twice that much time in case it runs long.

- **Do your homework.** Before the interview, research the organization and its people. Has the company been in the news? Has it struggled with any high-profile nurse turnover or safety and quality issues? Does the organization use a professional practice model for nursing, and is it Magnet designated?
- **Get ready to ask smart questions.** Write down what you want to know about the position, the organization's culture, the people you'd be working with and for, and so on. Beware of asking questions that are inappropriate at this stage, such as "What's the chance for promotion?" or "How many vacation days will I get?," because such questions can come across as presumptuous. Instead, ask smart questions. For example, "I read about your innovative patient-centered interprofessional care model. How did your team make it such a success?"
- **Be ready for old standby questions.** If asked "Can you tell me about yourself?," give a full picture but limit it to three minutes or less. Share some facts (e.g., education, family, geography), but also explain what your plan is, what your general professional hopes are, and why you're interviewing for that job in particular. If the interviewer asks, "What is your greatest weakness?," explain how you're compensating for that weakness. Avoid saying you work too hard or you're disorganized, which are two of the most clichéd answers. Good answers to such common questions show personal and professional awareness.
- **Know your stories.** Prepare eight to ten stories of two minutes or less that you can tap to answer behavioral questions, such as how you've used your leadership skills to solve problems at current or previous gigs. Use the S.O.A.R. method to frame your stories: a brief description of the *situation*, the *obstacles* you faced, the *action* you

took, and the *results* you achieved. Be prepared to explain what you learned from problems you have faced in your career. For example, "I left my secure job at a large healthcare system to take a job in a small home health company. It wasn't a good fit for me long-term, but I learned the importance of innovation in healthcare."

- **Know where you're going and how long it will take to get there.** There's nothing worse than getting lost or arriving late on interview day. Be sure you know where to report and what the parking situation is. Consider doing a dry run by visiting the site beforehand.
- **Dress your best** (see lesson 16). Conservative business dress is the order of the day. If you can afford it, purchase a new set of clothes to look and feel the part. Pay attention to the details—hair, shoes, fingernails, make-up, jewelry, and accessories should all be neat and business appropriate. Look like you care—your effort will shine through.

The interview itself is the next-to-last step before landing a job. You're nearly there! You'll want to arrive early (though not *too* early) to give yourself a chance to calm down on-site by waiting for a few minutes in the lobby or cafeteria. Go to the restroom and check your appearance. Be in the reception area at least five minutes early. Introduce yourself to everyone you meet, and do your level best to remember names.

Once the interview gets under way, the interviewer will be aiming to determine if you are the best candidate for the job and whether you'll be a productive, responsible, engaging, and motivated employee. Be prepared to explain why you want the job and why you're a good fit. Your answers should clearly demonstrate what skills you'll bring and how you'll add value.

- **Begin with a nice, firm handshake.** Repeat the name of each person you meet to cement it in your mind.

- **Let the interviewer show you where to sit.** Wait to be seated until you're invited to do so.
- **Exchange pleasantries.** Interviewers often begin with small talk. They may ask where you grew up and went to school. Let the interviewer take the lead. Use this opportunity to find a connection with the interviewer to help you relax.
- **Maintain good eye contact.** Look the interviewer in the eye, but without staring. If you're interviewing with a group, direct your gaze primarily at the person who asked the question but sweep your eyes around the table so that everyone feels addressed.
- **Manage anxiety.** Don't touch your face, fiddle with your hands, play with your hair, or otherwise fidget. You don't have to be stock-still, but keep the nervous movements under wraps.
- **Project energy and alertness throughout the interview.** Smiling occasionally will project a sense of confidence and ease. *Never* yawn or look bored. Let the interviewer know you're listening by nodding or murmuring occasionally.
- **Be concise and articulate.** Pause thoughtfully before answering each question. Breathe and relax as you talk. Avoid babbling by keeping each answer to under a minute unless the interviewer probes for more information. Don't go off on tangents, and *never* interrupt an interviewer. If you yourself are interrupted, take a moment to receive what is being said before replying.
- **If you don't understand a question, smile and ask for clarification.** Don't get stuck. Answer everything to the best of your ability, and remember that interview questions usually have no right or wrong answers. The interviewer wants to know how you handle pressure.
- **Don't inquire about salary and benefits unless the interviewer broaches the topic.** Be prepared to state

your preferred salary if asked, a number you've decided in advance to show you have a good idea of your worth. Don't be unrealistic; know what other people in similar positions make, and stay within or close to that range.

- **Keep up your side of the back-and-forth.** An interview is like a seesaw. Be prepared to ask as many questions as you need to during the process to understand the nature of the position and the culture of the company. You don't have to save all your questions until the end.

As the interview wraps up, finish strong. Summarize, in a sentence or two, why you would be a good hire for the company. Thank the interviewers for the chance to be considered. Let them know you're particularly interested in the job now that you've learned more about it and had a chance to meet the people you'll be working with.

Before you leave, ask about next steps. Do they hope to have someone in place within a few weeks? Within a few months? If you feel comfortable doing so, say, "May I phone or e-mail you next week?" Then give the interviewer a solid goodbye handshake. Thank the receptionist by name as you depart.

Afterward, send an e-mail note of thanks, which will give the interviewer an opportunity to respond. Handwritten thank-you notes are always a nice touch, but be sure to drop them in the mail either the same day or the following morning.

You may want to jot down notes for later reference. Make sure you write down the names and titles of the people you met correctly. What recurring themes did you perceive? What went well, and what didn't go as smoothly as you'd have liked?

You should always feel some anxiety over an interview; being nervous shows that you care. Practice and experience will mitigate such feelings to a certain extent, but if you don't feel a smidgen of nerves, consider why. Perhaps it's not a job you're interested in, or you've become a bit overconfident. Nervousness serves a purpose, and no one's beyond it. Try to find the right balance of being at ease and comfortable with presenting your best professional face.

EXERCISE 1

Write down eight to ten brief stories that illustrate how you have solved problems or handled difficult situations in the past. Keep them updated, and prepare new stories as you gain experience. Use the S.O.A.R. answer model to describe the situation, obstacles, action, and results.

EXERCISE 2

Conduct mock interviews with friends and counselors. Prepare a list of possible questions and practice answering them. Don't memorize the answers; answer them spontaneously, drawing on the stories you prepared in Exercise 1.

EXERCISE 3

Research every organization where you will have an interview. Try to gain an understanding of its culture and interviewing approach.

RESOURCES

Cattelan, L. 2016. "The S.O.A.R. Answer Model." Human Resources .com. Accessed November 26. www.humanresources.com/491 /the-soar-answer-model.

Job Interview Questions. 2016. "Ace Your Next Interview and Get the Job!" Accessed July 18. www.jobinterviewquestions.org.

Lehigh University. 2016. "S.T.A.R. Method for Behavioral Interviewing." Accessed November 11. http://careerservices.web.lehigh.edu/node/145.

Powers, P. 2010. *Winning Job Interviews*. Franklin Lakes, NJ: Career Press.

Ensure a Healthy Work Environment

Healthy work environments are driven by ongoing investment in skill building in communication, collaboration, and leadership; persistence and accountability in achieving a healthy new reality; and the courage to stand up for the rights and needs of patients and all members of the healthcare team.

—Kathy McCauley, PhD, RN, FAAN, FAHA, professor of cardiovascular nursing, University of Pennsylvania School of Nursing, Philadelphia, and president (2004–2005), American Association of Critical-Care Nurses

A HEALTHY WORK environment (HWE) is essential to a successful nursing career. Many nurse leaders champion an HWE in which *everyone* can flourish—nurses, other care providers, and patients and families.

Every nurse leader plays a role in creating an HWE as well as in nurturing and sustaining it. Most nurses know intuitively when they are working in an environment that is professional, that respects everyone, and that puts a focus on patient-centered care. And they know when their work is meaningful and appreciated.

Turning an unhealthy environment around can be a big assignment but is absolutely necessary. It takes courage and persistence. Unhealthy work environments can lead to conflict and stress among healthcare providers, unfortunate levels of organizational turnover, and—worst of all—unsafe care and poor patient outcomes. When nurse retention and engagement are significant concerns, nothing is more important than making an HWE happen.

So what exactly is an HWE? In 2005, to wide acclaim, the American Association of Critical-Care Nurses (AACN) first developed a set of six standards for establishing and sustaining HWEs. Updated in 2016, these standards underscore the importance of nurse retention to stem the tide of nurses leaving units, hospitals, and the profession and emphasize that issues such as disrespect and lack of effective communication can seriously harm the quality of care for patients and families. Just as important, the emotional lives of nurses and physicians are at risk as well. Moral distress—when a nurse knows the right thing to do but colleagues or policies get in the way—can create real heartbreak each and every day for nurses and nurse leaders.

The six AACN standards have stood the test of time:

1. **Skilled communication:** Nurses must be as proficient in communication skills as they are in clinical skills.
2. **True collaboration:** Nurses must be relentless in pursuing and fostering collaboration.
3. **Effective decision making:** Nurses must be valued and committed partners in making policy, directing and evaluating clinical care, and leading organizational operations.
4. **Appropriate staffing:** Staffing must ensure the effective match between patient needs and nurse competencies.
5. **Meaningful recognition:** Nurses must be recognized and must recognize others for the value each brings to the work of the organization [see lesson 34].
6. **Authentic leadership:** Nurse leaders must embrace the imperative of a healthy work environment, authentically live it, and engage others in its achievement.

As a nurse leader, you are responsible for creating, nurturing, and sustaining an HWE. So how do you do that? Here are a few tips:

- **Seek an HWE in all of your positions.** For their first work setting, new graduates should look for an environment that not only offers a strong clinical residency program but also espouses all six standards of an HWE. Magnet hospitals uphold many of these standards, as do hospital units that have won the AACN Beacon Award for Excellence.
- **Refer to the AACN standards for HWEs during job interviews.** Whether you're interviewing for a leadership position or for the next step on your career path, refer to the AACN standards and ask your prospective employer for examples of where the unit or organization aligns with them. Bring a copy of the standards to your interviews.
- **Assess your current environment.** How well does your current environment measure up to the AACN standards? If communication between nurses or between nurses and physicians is disrespectful, does the organization have a plan in place to address the problem? The landmark "Silence Kills" study showed that when nurses don't speak up about mistakes or gaps in care, patients can die (see lesson 12).
- **Make the AACN standards visible.** Post a copy of the AACN standards in a conspicuous place. Have conversations about the standards with your colleagues.
- **Offer to help make changes.** If you work in an unhealthy work environment, critically evaluate the environment's strengths and opportunities for improvement, and offer to help make changes where needed. Turnarounds are tough, but in many cases nurses have pulled together to change their environment and, in the process, created a stronger team spirit.

In turning an unhealthy work environment into a healthy one, nurses can become stronger leaders. And by paying attention to HWE strategies, it's even possible to turn a hospital that is struggling with nurse retention into one that has a waiting list!

EXERCISE 1

Consider your various experiences as a nurse. What were the best jobs you held, and what organizations offered the healthiest work environments? Compare these jobs and organizations to the AACN standards for HWEs.

EXERCISE 2

Use the AACN survey to assess whether your unit or organization qualifies as an HWE: www.aacn.org/nursing-excellence /healthy-work-environments.

RESOURCES

American Association of Critical-Care Nurses (AACN). 2016. *AACN Standards for Establishing and Sustaining Healthy Work Environments: A Journey to Excellence*, 2nd ed. www.aacn.org/wd/hwe /docs/hwestandards.pdf.

Maxfield, D., J. Grenny, R. McMillan, K. Patterson, and A. Switzler. 2005. *Silence Kills: The Seven Crucial Conversations for Healthcare.* VitalSmarts and American Association of Critical-Care Nurses. Accessed July 24, 2016. www.aacn.org/WD/Practice/Docs /PublicPolicy/SilenceKills.pdf.

Ulrich, B. T., R. Lavandero, D. Woods, and S. Early. 2014. "Critical Care Nurse Work Environments 2013: A Status Report." *Critical Care Nurse* 34 (4): 64–79.

Handle Failures and Disappointments

I have experienced failure on more than one occasion during my leadership journey. Whether it was expected or it caught me completely off guard, I was usually struck by an overwhelming sense of disappointment. As leaders, we know that failures can teach us important lessons and do not define us. Handling failures and disappointments is easier when you maintain a focused strategy and view them as temporary setbacks that can be overcome if you just keep pushing. Failures offer us opportunities to slow down—maybe even pause—but eventually to push through and rise above. I'm a better leader not because of my failures and disappointments but because of how I've responded.

—Dave Hanson, MSN, RN, ACNS-BC, NEA-BC, regional director of nursing practice, education, and professional development, Providence Health & Services Southern California, Burbank, California, and president (2007–2008), American Association of Critical-Care Nurses

IT GOES WITHOUT saying that you'll have failures and disappointments in your life—no human alive is untouched by adversity. You'll be at the helm of failed projects; miss opportunities; experience mishaps with colleagues, supervisors, and patients; lose jobs; and suffer a host of personal losses. It's just part of life.

Because problems in life are guaranteed, the bigger question is how you'll handle them. Will you blame others for issues beyond your control? Will difficulties scare you away from thinking creatively and taking risks? Will they create undue fear and anxiety? Or will you learn and grow as a result of your failures? The most seasoned leaders know that dealing with setbacks right away is one key to being successful. When bad stuff happens, the most effective leaders are able to handle difficulties in the moment and in the hours and days after, synthesizing what didn't work to strengthen their process of discovering what *does* work for tasks down the line.

The strongest people turn failures into opportunities, put the past behind them, and focus on their future direction. Distinguishing between failures and setbacks may be helpful; according to mindfulness guru Deepak Chopra, MD, a setback is temporary and surmountable, whereas failure leaves a scar and induces fear, anxiety, and—worst of all—inertia. Thus, it's crucial not to let short-term setbacks turn into long-term failures. If you accept that idea, you can overcome almost anything.

Often, the best salve is close at hand and involves keeping busy, moving, and engaged. As a nurse leader, you are part of a core group of individuals who help people in need—and that reminder alone is powerful motivation and inspiration when times get tough. If your professional life has become sodden with controversy or you're in the thick of a setback, you might turn to family or faith, but you could also work at a local free clinic or volunteer on a hospital unit that needs a hand. Bring yourself up by bringing yourself back to the core reason you do what you do—this alone can put you on a path to recovery.

No problem lasts forever. Stay as positive as you can, focusing on today and what you can do to move forward. And don't forget to forgive yourself for making mistakes. Be transparent, own your error, and then forgive yourself. View yourself as worthy and successful no matter what is happening. Inspirational speaker and researcher Brené Brown stresses the importance of letting go of perfectionism and what people think to truly allow yourself to shine. If you believe wholeheartedly that you'll find your route to recovery, it will soon be true.

Here are some ideas to temper failures and disappointments:

- **Keep expectations reasonable.** Not everything you do can or will be great. Conversely, if you're achieving all you set out to do, you've probably set the bar too low. Stretch to achieve more difficult goals, even if success isn't always in the bag. Difficult successes are much more satisfying than easy ones.

- **Get comfortable with risk** (see lesson 2). Take on new tasks with the understanding that you may experience setbacks. If you're offered a job that is a stretch, don't count all the reasons you might get stuck—take it. You may do better than you expect and, despite mistakes, may learn a great deal. Most successful entrepreneurs assert that they derived their greatest success from what came *after* abject failure.

- **Analyze what happened.** Talk to your colleagues to get the whole picture, being sure to own your part in what went wrong. Is your skill set weak? How is your emotional intelligence? Are your interpersonal skills lackluster? Are others not pulling their weight? Perhaps coaching, professional development, or education will improve your (or your staff's) next try. If your deficits are offset by the talents of certain staffers, get their help on the next project. Great leaders surround themselves with people whose strengths complement their weaknesses.

- **Talk about it, but not endlessly.** You're not the first one to bomb a presentation before the board, to butt heads with a boss, or to get fired. Plenty of colleagues and friends in your network have felt the same sorrows and frustrations. Talk to them about it, but not forever. Know when you've talked it through and then move on.

- **Don't brood.** Take the "where to from here?" approach. Getting past failures can take time, but don't spend weeks lamenting a disappointing outcome. At some point, it's imperative that you press on—changed, better informed, and ready for what's next.
- **Hire people who have tried hard and failed.** Smart managers examine applicants both on their own merits and in the context of their work. People who try and fail are braver and far better bets than those who have followed traditional paths, never taken risks, and earned easy successes as a result.

As you make your way out of the morass of a large problem, do your best not to repeat your mistakes. If you find yourself making the same errors repeatedly, you may need the help of a mentor or professional coach. But if you're thoughtful about your experiences and are able to tap your own reservoir of self-worth and value, you'll pull through a lifetime's worth of setbacks. There's not one of them that you won't be able to topple.

EXERCISE 1

Write down what you consider important in your life. Understanding who you are will help you deal with loss and failure.

EXERCISE 2

If something went wrong, whom would you turn to? Whom can you talk with about problems? Make a list of people in your support group.

RESOURCES

Brown, B. 2010. *The Gifts of Imperfection: Let Go of Who You Think You're Supposed to Be and Embrace Who You Are*. Center City, MN: Hazelden.

Chopra, D. 2013. "How to Protect Yourself from Failure." LinkedIn. Posted November 23. www.linkedin.com/today/post /article/20131123022336-75054000-how-to-protect-yourself -from-failure.

Godin, S. 2007. *The Dip: A Little Book That Teaches You When to Quit (and When to Stick)*. New York: Penguin Group.

Plews-Ogan, M., J. E. Owens, and N. May. 2012. *Choosing Wisdom: Strategies and Inspiration for Growing Through Life-Changing Difficulties*. West Conshohocken, PA: Templeton Press.

Balance Life and Work

There is no such thing as work–life balance. There is only life—your life—and you only get one life to live. Time is a commodity, and there's a limited amount. Think of it like money: Be strategic about how you spend it, and only invest it in what you really care about. Block regular time on your calendar for "me time"—unstructured downtime, think time, and fun time. As a leader, if you're not having fun, you can't be at your best. Keeping you happy will benefit everyone. Once your calendar is full, it's time to say no. If it's hard to say no, then say, "I can't take that on now—maybe later."

—Emily Drake, PhD, RN, FAAN, professor, University of Virginia School of Nursing, Charlottesville, and president (2017), Association of Women's Health, Obstetrics and Neonatal Nurses

NURSING IS IMPORTANT work, and people's very lives are affected by the decisions we nurses make. Given the profession's demands on our time and energy, it's important to think long and hard about your personal priorities and to strike a balance between life and work. Despite the rigors of the field, with a little effort you *can* achieve some degree of balance, if not total equity.

The following questions will guide you as you consider a hospital, academic, or leadership position in nursing:

- **Do I work to live or live to work?** Be honest with yourself: Are you looking for a professional challenge, or do you want stability and a paycheck?
- **What's most important to me?** Make an honest list tallying where work, family, and hobbies rank in your life. Is coaching your son's soccer team a top priority? What about having solitary time with your dog in the park every afternoon? Do you need to continue competitive cycling or running to keep yourself sane? Put it on the list. Your career will likely require trade-offs, so knowing what ranks where is critical.
- **How does my family fit in?** You won't have endless chances to attend your daughter's birthday celebrations, your son's kindergarten play, or your kids' first recitals because children grow up fast. And you'd be smart to have frank and open discussions about your career with your partner or spouse, especially if he or she has a good job or if the relationship would crumble if you're working too many night shifts or you're in the office too much. Your personal relationships should be far more important than your job, unless you want to look back on your career and see a string of losses.
- **What's the hospital or company culture?** If you're considering a job at a new organization, talk to people who work there to get an idea of whether it offers the work–life balance you seek. Is it a "get the job done and go home" kind of place? Or one that will require long hours because of staffing levels, innovations that have no charted path, and large projects and initiatives on the horizon? If you're willing to go for the latter, remember that the rewards may be large but are mainly professional. Consider what's best for you, especially if you have a family, partner, or lifestyle that requires dedicated time away from the office.
- **How much travel is required?** For certain nurse leader positions—such as those in consulting and health system

corporate offices—significant travel may be involved. Travel can have a real impact on your personal life and cut into your ability to enjoy routine pastimes. Given that organizations often underestimate the amount of time employees travel, it's up to you to get a full picture of what will be required. Remember to build in time to travel to and from airports and hotels and to change planes. Also consider that a one-hour meeting in another city just a quick plane ride away can turn into a three-day trip if inclement weather or a complication arises.

- **What about weekends and flexibility?** Many healthcare organizations that require significant travel or weekend work allow some degree of reciprocal flex time, but as a manager, your presence in the office is likely needed. Some managers set the tone in their office by leaving consistently at 5:00 p.m., whereas others are the last to leave. Know that your patterns in the office will affect how others perceive your diligence and effort. Researchers have found that those who arrive and end their day early tend to be considered less hardworking than those who start later and stay late—even if the total number of hours worked is the same. If you consistently leave early to tend to children, a hobby, or a relationship, those who keep more traditional hours may look at you askance. The same goes for working from home. Early on in your career, expect to put in long days to gain experience, credibility, and the respect of your colleagues.

Consider these additional ideas to help you strike the right balance:

- **Learn to say no politely but firmly.** Many people commit to new tasks without really thinking about how it will affect their home life. Learn not to take on new obligations without talking it over with your family first. If you're already tapped out, shed or delegate another of your tasks before agreeing to take on a new one.

- **Trim your to-do list.** Review your commitments and, if possible, eliminate activities that you do not enjoy or that someone else can tackle.
- **Dedicate time to unplug.** Disconnecting periodically will enable you to be present when you need to be (see lesson 8) so that you can truly engage with the task or people before you.
- **Work smarter.** Cut time wasters from your life (see lesson 3). Don't flit from assignment to assignment in a disorganized, inefficient manner. Be organized, and keep an organized office (see lesson 22). Make sure you understand assignments before you start them, and learn to batch errands so that you can cut down on the number of trips you take.
- **Be your own master.** Control your schedule to the extent you can.

You alone are responsible for finding the right work–life balance. Although companies and technology allow greater flexibility than ever before, nothing replaces old-fashioned face time and long hours—especially when you're the manager, and especially early in your career. Working smartly and efficiently and dedicating time during your day to focus your full attention on nonwork activities are good places to begin. If you set boundaries, your work colleagues will generally respect them. If not, it may be time for a change.

EXERCISE 1

Make a list of the activities that you least enjoy, and consider dropping them.

EXERCISE 2

Have regular meetings with your family. Discuss with them your work and what you value the most on a routine basis.

RESOURCES

Groysberg, B., and R. Abrahams. 2014. "Manage Your Work, Manage Your Life." *Harvard Business Review* 92 (3): 58–66.

Mayo Clinic. 2012. "Work–Life Balance: Tips to Reclaim Control." Published July 12. www.mayoclinic.org/work-life-balance/art -20048134.

Sandberg, S. 2013. *Lean In: Women, Work, and the Will to Lead.* New York: Knopf.

Uscher, J. 2013. "5 Tips for Better Work–Life Balance." Web MD. Posted March 28. www.webmd.com/health-insurance /protect-health-13/balance-life.

LESSON 48

Commit to Lifelong Learning

Lifelong learning is a continuous process of seeking answers to questions and addressing the personal and professional conundrums that form the fabric of competence and expertise.

—Jann T. Balmer, PhD, RN, FACEHP, director of continuing medical education, University of Virginia School of Medicine, Charlottesville; continuing education co-lead nurse planner, University of Virginia School of Nursing, Charlottesville; and chair (2014–2017), Commission on Accreditation, American Nurses Credentialing Center

AT NO POINT in your career—or your life, frankly—should you feel that you've somehow learned it all. The best, most authentic leaders commit to a curriculum of lifelong learning throughout their careers to keep current and stay relevant. While your formal education provides you with a regimented knowledge base at the outset, the field of healthcare management is in near-constant flux. That means you will learn many of your most critical lessons naturally, on the job, as you contemplate and solve real-world problems.

But even the richest on-the-job experiences don't offer you everything you need to learn and grow. Seek help from mentors, coaches, and bosses to keep current and to turn any personal or educational deficits you have into strengths. And be dogged about consuming information wherever, whenever, and as regularly as you can. Only *you* can drive that.

Here are a few tips to guide ongoing learning:

- **Read avidly.** Keep reading material on your bedside table, in your briefcase, and in your bathroom. Invest in subscriptions to magazines and journals related to your field. Read at least two books and two professional journals every month. Discuss the books with those in your network who share your interests, being sure to get their book recommendations. The more you read, the richer your ideas will become.
- **Set goals for self-improvement.** Your focus on what to improve skills- and knowledge-wise will shift from time to time. You can always boost your competence in certain areas. If you are afraid to speak in public, for example, you might improve your proficiency by joining a local Toastmasters club. You might then volunteer to speak at small events, churches, or social clubs. As you gain confidence, you might seek more challenging venues.
- **Keep going.** Once you have mastered a new skill, start anew. Have you conquered public speaking? Aim to become a better writer. Want to hone your business communication skills? Take a course in crucial conversations so that you've got strategies to tap when facing a difficult interaction with a colleague or direct report.
- **Keep abreast of current strategies.** Learn everything you can about quality improvement techniques, such as Lean and Six Sigma, and strategies used to reduce waste and solve problems. Attend training programs that can expand your skill set in identifying activities that aren't adding value to your organization.
- **Take others with you.** As you widen your knowledge and understanding of best healthcare business practices,

include the right mix of colleagues and stakeholders who, together, can help you focus on a problem and solve it. If multiple colleagues might benefit from a course or retreat, invite them to attend such seminars together.

- **Aim to become an expert.** When a subject piques your interest, consume everything you can on the topic. Books, journal articles, websites, blogs—have a voracious appetite. Being intensely interested in a subject makes it easier to consume, digest, and share what you know.

- **Learn what others do.** Soak up what you can from those whose jobs are different from yours. If a physician performs a new procedure, for example, express curiosity and ask to observe. Find out what other nursing or healthcare organizations are doing so that you can understand what their best practices are. You might be able to mimic their strategies back home.

- **Be professionally malleable.** Once upon a time, it was a straight shot from charge nurse to nurse manager or supervisor and—after attainment of a master's degree—to a director or chief nurse position. But today, because of growth and change, such a career trajectory is no longer the case. Consider other professional aspects of nursing leadership that might be outside your comfort zone. Having a breadth of knowledge is positive for career advancement. You might consider a lateral move or a position in a different organization or country to widen the scope of your understanding and experience. Stretch yourself—take on assignments you might never have imagined for yourself. Take a job that you know very little about, and then master it. You'll be the better for it. (And don't limit yourself to jobs at the nurse executive level. Nurses in C-suite positions are highly valued and sought for their leadership expertise and knowledge of clinical and strategic operations.)

- **Affiliate with a professional association.** Become active in your nursing specialty organization. In addition, organizations such as the American Organization of Nurse Executives, the American College of Healthcare Executives, and the American Nurses Credentialing Center have missions to improve the knowledge of their members and offer venues for continuing education. Attend their conferences and webinars, read their blogs, and join their social media and LinkedIn groups.

The bottom line? Don't sit still. The best future nurse leaders leaders are those who bring a rich variety of skills and experiences to the table and whose appetites for knowledge and growth are never satiated. Executives who have worked in multiple settings and who are professionally malleable will always be in high demand because they're flexible and can adapt quickly to new challenges. They are the people companies want and need.

So even if it's out of your comfort zone, go for a position that stretches you in an area that will broaden your knowledge and experience base in acute care, ambulatory care, care coordination, nursing informatics, managed care, quality improvement, or finance. You'll learn a great deal about large and complex healthcare systems, you'll tackle issues you might never have imagined—and you and your career will be the better for it.

EXERCISE 1

In your professional development plan, you indicated gaps in your competencies and areas that need strengthening. Find continuing education opportunities or other ways to turn those weaknesses into strengths.

EXERCISE 2

Attend the annual Congress on Healthcare Leadership of the American College of Healthcare Executives or the annual meeting of the American Organization of Nurse Executives. Attend the career development programs, and complete the instruments there that will help you develop a plan for lifelong learning.

RESOURCES

American College of Healthcare Executives. 2017. "About ACHE." Accessed February 9. www.ache.org.

American Organization of Nurse Executives. 2017. "AONE Education Programs." Accessed February 9. www.aone.org/education /overview.shtml.

Discern When It's Time to Leave

*My decisions to leave a job were always hard because I was fortunate
to have talented coworkers, but healthcare always presented new
challenges. I wanted to engage in policy—to improve access to care—
and to deal with affordability and quality. So the itch to change may
be about wanting to experience your field from a different point of
view. Applying different skills that you have acquired over the years
can also be very rewarding.*

—Marilyn Tavenner, MHA, RN, president and CEO,
America's Health Insurance Plans, Washington, DC

HEALTHCARE IS EXPERIENCING tumultuous times, but change
and financial challenges are hardly limited to our profession. *Every*
manager should be prepared to change jobs numerous times during
his or her career. And even if you love the job you're in, you should
always have your hoped-for career trajectory and professional development plan in mind (see lesson 41) and be open to opportunities
that arise.

When it's time to go, always leave on the best terms possible. The
world is small, and the person you rudely cut off in traffic today or
speak disparagingly about to a friend might be your connection to
your next big job. Never burn bridges.

An old adage quips, "It's better to leave six months too early than
six months too late." The difficulty, of course, is knowing whether

you've overstayed a job. You don't have to keep one foot out the door at all times, but remain flexible and be prepared to move if things deteriorate beyond repair. Before you leave a job, evaluate your career plans; talk to your mentors and family; and carefully consider all of the factors that will affect your decision, including emotional and financial ones. And always remember that it is much easier to find a job while you still have one.

So how do you know when it's time to go? Ask yourself these questions:

- **Why do I want to leave my job?** The answer to this question should take less than two minutes to express, be on the tip of your tongue, and not require deep contemplation. Are your reasons rational, or are they emotional? Are you getting signs that it is time to go—for example, are you receiving fewer invitations to key meetings or have you stopped receiving them altogether? Have you stopped learning new skills? Do you dread going to work every day? Do the negatives about your job outweigh the positives?

- **Do I feel consistently unhappy at work?** Life changes—for example, a birth, a death, a divorce, or a move—sometimes spur professional discontent. Are you truly unhappy, or are you just in a funk? Is your current job the source of your unhappiness, or is it a mere bystander to it? Does work make you unhappy because of its time demands and excessive travel and because it separates you from your family? And if so, is it worth scrapping the entire job, or should you attempt to shift the way you do it?

- **What effect will changing jobs have on my career?** Think about how it will look on your resume. You do not want to be perceived as a job hopper. If you want to leave because you're having trouble meeting expectations, try to work through those problems—by doing so, you will learn and grow.

- **What will I do next?** You should have a solid concept of what comes next that you can articulate in two minutes or less.
- **How would changing jobs affect my family?** This question is important. Think practically. How does your spouse feel about you making a change? Can you sell your house? Where will you live? Will your partner need to get a job or work more hours to cover costs? Where will your children go to school? How important is living close to your extended family? Will the new position you seek require more travel and time away from home?
- **Are there solid reasons to stay?** Your current position should be part of your career plan and among the career goals you set for yourself to accomplish. Are there other, unfinished goals that you can still attain in your current role? Have you expressed interest in a promotion, or do you know or sense you're on the shortlist for one? Does your name come up when your company has an opening?
- **Am I sure the change will be an improvement?** Some young executives leave a good position early on for a tantalizing increase in pay only to find that they are worse off in the new position. Such pathways can derail your career. If something is not right in your current position, make your feelings known before you decide to leave. Discuss your situation with your boss and with the right people in human resources. State your concerns clearly—don't expect people to guess the source of your unhappiness. Explain what you think you need to be successful in your current role. You might be surprised how positively senior management responds.

Whatever the situation, your departure should be positive and professional. Be gracious when you leave a position—even if you've been fired—and do your best to leave on friendly terms. Healthcare is a smaller field than you might imagine, and you will likely cross paths with former colleagues time and time again.

Once you decide to leave, own your decision—don't look back or second-guess yourself. Every decision has degrees of good and bad. Over the course of our careers, we all end up in bad situations, in jobs that are a poor professional match, or in positions where we make mistakes. We're only human. But when one door closes, another one opens. Will you be ready for what's next?

EXERCISE 1

Keep your professional development plan and your resume current (see lessons 41 and 42), and make sure your network is robust and up to date (see lesson 43). If you were fired tomorrow, what would you do?

EXERCISE 2

Create a personal financial plan. Save enough cash to pay your bills for at least six months if you are not working.

RESOURCE

Tyler, J. L. 2011. *Tyler's Guide: The Healthcare Executive's Job Search*, 4th ed. Chicago: Health Administration Press.

Find Your Next Job

Nurses are blessed to have an abundance of career opportunities. The challenge sometimes is deciding when in your career you should transition to a new position. Sometimes the change is required—your spouse is relocating, for example, or you're asked to change roles. But usually the choice is yours, and the decision can be hard. If you are feeling a subtle restlessness, it may be a signal to start your job search. Focus on what would keep you engaged and interested and help you feel you are making your optimal contribution. Always be open to new possibilities, and don't be afraid of new challenges that may stretch you in ways you never imagined. A straight career trajectory is rare; more often, a job takes twists and turns that ultimately lead to an exciting new position and a rewarding career.

—Patricia Gonce Morton, PhD, RN, ACNP-BC, FAAN, dean and professor, Louis H. Peery Presidential Endowed Chair, University of Utah College of Nursing, Salt Lake City

AN IMPORTANT PART of *any* successful career is the ability to find and transition into a new job when the time comes. Many executives have made successful moves that ignited their careers. Others have relied on a series of lateral moves before breaking into the upper echelons of their profession. If you've established a robust network and acquired the range of skills you need to take your work life to the next level, your chances for success will be much higher.

A successful job search has several key components:

- Plan and focus.
- Project confidence and keep a positive attitude.
- Define your brand and know what sets you apart.
- Keep a daily activity level that is consistent with your situation. If you do not have a job, your full-time job is to find one.

In the event you are terminated, you may need time to emotionally process the experience before refocusing your efforts on searching for a new job. Most people need time to grieve after they are fired, particularly if they held a position for a long time, and won't be ready to move on until they've come to terms with the loss. If your every thought begins with how you were professionally mistreated, you likely haven't gotten over it. Attempt to understand what went wrong, *own your part in it*, and aim to pull yourself out of what happened better informed—and ready to find a stronger professional match with your skills.

Your network can help with job searches, of course, but beware: When you're looking for a new job, the connections you approach—whether they are personal or professional—are usually not interested in hearing about what happened at your old one. Keep the details about what happened to no more than a couple of sentences: "It wasn't a good match" or "I felt the pull of other opportunities." Don't talk trash about places and people, because the world can be awfully small.

Starting fresh gives you a chance to think long and hard about what you'd like to do next. Consider what you loved about previous jobs, as well as what aspects didn't excite you as much. Knowing what you want out of a job—and what you have to offer—is a great first step toward focusing your efforts.

Follow these steps for a successful job search:

1. **Write a professional development plan to focus your efforts** (see lesson 41). This plan will help you recognize

your strengths, identify target organizations, and begin your networking efforts. Then list 20 places where you'd like to work. Keep your list dynamic—if you cross off a hospital, university, or company that is no longer a contender, replace it with another.

2. **Update your resume** (see lesson 42). Seek help from a mentor, a human resources professional, or other experts. If you get conflicting advice from different sources, let your inner voice tell you which advice to follow. Don't spend too much time on your resume's content because, although important, a resume is only a tool. It's who you are, what you offer, and your professional experiences— not endless wordsmithing—that will land you the job. Get your resume set, and then begin pounding the pavement.

3. **Begin networking within and around your list of top 20 organizations** (see lesson 43). After you identify the positions that fit your levels of education and experience, attempt to understand each organization's structure. Who does the hiring? Which of your contacts has some link to that person? Even tangential relationships can open the door a crack. Submitting a formal application will make you just another applicant in a teeming sea of qualified and unqualified hopefuls. Your network can help you stand out, upping the chances that you'll get in the door for an interview.

   A word of caution: Don't rely solely on e-mail and the Internet to land a job. You'll need to reach out and meet with people every day. Unnerving as personal contacts can be, even a follow-up cold call (practiced beforehand, of course) is better than a tiresome e-mail with attachments that may never be opened. Show you care by putting yourself out there—you'll be among the few who do.

4. **Practice and prepare for initial screenings that may be conducted by phone.** Coach yourself, cultivate your telephone demeanor, and jot down a few short, succinct

bullet points about your personal brand so that you'll be prepared, even if you're given only a few moments.

5. **Take time to fully prepare for your face-to-face interview**, the most important part of the job search (see lesson 44). Be ready to show how you can solve the company's problems, projecting energy as you explain why the job is a good fit for you and how you'll add remarkable value to the company. Even if you don't get the offer straightaway, you'll leave a lasting impression if you do well and may be remembered and considered for other positions that arise. Never burn bridges—be respectful and act like a grown-up even when you *don't* land the job.

6. **Balance aggressiveness in your job search with professionalism and courtesy.** If your call or e-mail has not been returned, follow up—but use good judgment to make sure you are coming across as persistent and interested, not as irritating, angry, or pushy.

7. **Know how to receive a job offer and negotiate your salary.** Your goal is to obtain viable job offers. Never withdraw your application from consideration (you can always turn down an offer once it has been extended), and wait until you've received an offer in writing before you make a decision. Know your worth in the market, consider what nonmonetary benefits the new position will afford— and then negotiate in good faith to achieve a fair salary.

Among the most critical components of a job search is keeping your spirits up despite some inevitable setbacks. Keep your emotions steady and remain focused. Focus, prepare, and move!

EXERCISE 1

Set a goal to write your professional development plan, finish your resume, and begin networking within the next 30 days. If you're conducting a job search while unemployed, set and achieve specific, daily goals. Commit to making a specific number of calls and network connections each day as well as to sending your resume out to a certain number of organizations. Read up on organizations you're targeting to get a full sense of what they're like, what their priorities are, and what directions they're moving in.

EXERCISE 2

Develop and work with your network. Actively strive to meet with people each day. Most executive jobs come from networking.

RESOURCES

Aldrich, J. 2013. *Climbing the Healthcare Management Ladder: Career Advice from the Top on What It Takes to Succeed*. Baltimore, MD: Health Professions Press.

American College of Healthcare Executives. 2016. "Careers." Accessed July 31. www.healthmanagementcareers.org/careers .cfm.

American Organization of Nurse Executives. 2016. "Career Center." Accessed July 31. http://careers.aone.org.

About the Authors

Kenneth R. White, PhD, AGACNP, ACHPN, FACHE, FAAN, is the University of Virginia (UVA) Medical Center endowed professor of nursing and associate dean for strategic partnerships and innovation in the School of Nursing. He also holds faculty appointments in the UVA School of Medicine, Darden School of Business, and McIntire School of Commerce.

Ken has more than 40 years' experience in healthcare organizations in clinical, administrative, governance, and consulting capacities. He spent 13 years with Mercy Health Services as a senior executive in marketing, operations, and international healthcare consulting. From 1995 to 2001, Ken was associate director of the master of health administration (MHA) and master of science in health administration programs at Virginia Commonwealth University (VCU), and from 2001 to 2008, he was director of VCU's master of health administration and dual degree (MHA/MD and MHA/JD) programs. He served from 2006 to 2009 as VCU's first Charles P. Cardwell, Jr., Professor and from 2012 to 2013 as VCU's inaugural Sentara Healthcare Professor of Health Administration.

Ken is a board-certified acute care nurse practitioner with specialty board certification in palliative care. He is a Fellow of the American Academy of Nursing as well as a Fellow, former Regent, and former member of the Board of Governors of the American College of Healthcare Executives (ACHE). In 2016, Ken became the founding chair of ACHE's LGBT Forum. He holds a visiting professor appointment at the LUISS Guido Carli University in Rome, Italy.

Ken received a PhD in health services organization and research from VCU. He earned an MPH in health administration at the University of Oklahoma, an MS in nursing at VCU, and a post-master's certificate in the acute care nurse practitioner program at UVA. He has extensive experience in hospital administration and consulting, particularly in the areas of leadership development, marketing, facility planning, palliative care program development, and operations management.

He is the author (with John R. Griffith) of *The Well-Managed Healthcare Organization*, fifth, sixth, seventh, and eighth editions; *Thinking Forward: Six Strategies for Successful Organizations*; and *Reaching Excellence in Healthcare Management* (all published by Health Administration Press). He is also the author (with J. Stephen Lindsey) of *Take Charge of Your Healthcare Management Career: 50 Lessons That Drive Success* (Health Administration Press). He is a contributing author to *Human Resources in Healthcare: Managing for Success*, fourth edition (Health Administration Press), *Fundamentals of Human Resources in Healthcare* (Health Administration Press), *Advances in Health Care Organization Theory* (Jossey-Bass), *Perianesthesia Nursing: A Critical Care Approach* (Saunders), *Introduction to Health Services* (Delmar), *Evidence-Based Management in Healthcare* (Health Administration Press), and *Managerial Ethics in Healthcare: A New Perspective* (Health Administration Press).

In 2013, Ken was named one of 120 Visionary Leaders as part of VCU School of Nursing's 120th anniversary celebration. He received the ACHE Edgar C. Hayhow Award for Article of the Year in 2006 and the James A. Hamilton Award for Book of the Year in 2012. He has served on several hospital, health system, and community nonprofit boards.

Ken lives in Afton, Virginia, with his husband, Dr. Carl Outen.

Dorrie K. Fontaine, PhD, RN, FAAN, has served since 2008 as dean of the School of Nursing at the University of Virginia (UVA), where she is the Sadie Heath Cabaniss Professor of Nursing and associate chief nursing officer at the UVA Medical Center. The founder of UVA's Compassionate Care Initiative, Dorrie has more than 40 years' experience as a critical care and trauma nurse and a distinguished record of leadership at the nation's top nursing schools, including those of the University of Maryland; Georgetown University; and the University of California, San Francisco. She is a tireless champion of creating healthy work environments, training nurses and physicians together, and developing resilient nurses and healthcare leaders through compassionate care.

Dorrie believes that nurturing resilience, teaching compassion, and augmenting wisdom through mindful leadership will truly transform the cultures of both clinical and academic healthcare settings. Her award-winning textbook coauthored with Patricia Gonce Morton, *Critical Care Nursing: A Holistic Approach* (Wolters Kluwer Health), is now in its tenth edition. Dorrie presents and publishes on compassion and mindfulness, as well as leadership, to interprofessional audiences.

Dorrie is a past president of the American Association of Critical-Care Nurses and the current president of the Virginia Association of Colleges of Nursing. She earned a BSN from Villanova University, an MS from the University of Maryland, and a PhD from the Catholic University of America. Inducted as a Fellow of the American Academy of Nursing in 1995, she received both the Presidential Citation from the Society of Critical Care Medicine and a Medallion for Contributions to the Profession from Villanova University in 1999. She received the Distinguished Alumni Award from the University of Maryland in 2012 and the Dr. Martin Luther King, Jr., UVA Health System Award for championing diversity and inclusion in 2015.

She lives in Pavilion IX, one of the ten pavilions designed by Thomas Jefferson on UVA's historic lawn, with her husband Barry.